# How Executives Should Think About AI

Much of what is said about AI is misleading – or just plain wrong. It's also sometimes intended to frighten everyone about a future that's unlikely to occur (think Bill Gates, Elon Musk, Steve Wozniak and Geoffrey Hinton, among others). AI will not steal children, hold hostages for bitcoins or start nuclear wars. But it *will* fundamentally change business through the intelligent automation of many routine – *and nonroutine* – tasks that companies perform all the time. Old business models will die as fast as new ones emerge. Whole industries will be reengineered, reinvented and reimagined. Some will be displaced altogether. Some industries will be disrupted in every sense of the word – in just three-to-five years. In fact, it's already begun.

*How Executives Should Think About AI: Straight Talk About the Inevitable* prepares executives for the AI future. It's not a complicated treatise on AI, or a theoretical look at how new technology can transform business models and processes. It's a series of conversations masquerading as chapters designed to help executives quickly understand AI, what it can do and what they should do about AI, machine learning (ML) and generative AI (GenAI) right now. These conversations about AI are intended to get executives up to speed on AI, ML and GenAI so that they become "AI comfortable" in many ways, including launching a steady stream of demonstration prototypes to help their companies explore AI's capabilities and potential benefits.

These timely conversations can help executives understand how AI will impact their companies and their professional success. It's straight talk about the most important technology since the Internet. Executives have no choice but to embrace AI to accomplish their professional goals. This book helps accomplish these goals. It helps them make decisions about what AI can and cannot do for their companies.

**Stephen J. Andriole's** career has focused on the development, application and management of information technology and analytical methodology to problems in government and industry. Dr. Andriole has addressed them from academia, government, his own consulting companies, a global insurance and financial services company, a pharmaceutical company, the perspective of a public venture operating company, a private equity venture capitalist, a corporate director and an Angel investor. The focus of his career has been on technology innovation, the optimization and management of technology, and technology adoption, deployment and governance. He has pioneered the application of AI and ML, interactive systems design, technology due diligence and the tracking and application of emerging business technologies.

# How Executives Should Think About AI

Straight Talk About the Inevitable

Stephen J. Andriole

CRC Press
Taylor & Francis Group
Boca Raton  London  New York

CRC Press is an imprint of the
Taylor & Francis Group, an **informa** business

AN AUERBACH BOOK

First edition published 2026
2385 NW Executive Center Drive, Suite 320, Boca Raton FL 33431

and by CRC Press
4 Park Square, Milton Park, Abingdon, Oxon, OX14 4RN

*CRC Press is an imprint of Taylor & Francis Group, LLC*

© 2026 Stephen J. Andriole

Reasonable efforts have been made to publish reliable data and information, but the author and publisher cannot assume responsibility for the validity of all materials or the consequences of their use. The authors and publishers have attempted to trace the copyright holders of all material reproduced in this publication and apologize to copyright holders if permission to publish in this form has not been obtained. If any copyright material has not been acknowledged please write and let us know so we may rectify in any future reprint.

ISBN: 9781041097983 (hbk)
ISBN: 9781041100218 (pbk)
ISBN: 9781003652748 (ebk)

DOI: 10.1201/9781003652748

Typeset in Times
by Newgen Publishing UK

# Contents

# Introduction

---

## HOW EXECUTIVES SHOULD THINK ABOUT AI

---

You don't have a lot of time. You run a business. You make lots of decisions every day. But "AI" is everywhere, all the time. So how should you think about AI? What decisions should you make regarding what AI can and cannot do for your company?

Let's remember that much of what you hear about AI is misleading – or just plain wrong. It's also sometimes intended to frighten you about a future that's unlikely to occur (think Bill Gates, Elon Musk, Steve Wozniak and Geoffrey Hinton, among others). AI will not steal your kids, hold you hostage for bitcoins or start nuclear wars. But it *will* fundamentally change your business through the intelligent automation of many routine – *and nonroutine* – tasks you and your company perform all the time. Old business models will die as fast as new ones emerge. Whole industries will be reengineered, reinvented and reimagined. Some will disappear altogether. Maybe even yours.

Those who make decisions about the relationship between AI and their companies have to get this right: AI is – *no kidding* – the most important technology in a generation.

AI, machine learning (ML) and generative AI (GenAI) will displace your knowledge workers – *your well-educated professionals* – in finance, accounting, human resources, consulting, marketing, transportation, manufacturing, healthcare, entertainment, real estate – you name the industry. In fact, every industry will be impacted by AI in ways you cannot precisely describe today. Your industry will not escape the tsunami. I don't care what kind of industry it is. While it's impossible to predict exactly when the bombs will explode, they will explode in a few years – not ten. While no one can tell you how many of your employees will be unnecessary, the number will be meaningful. 20%? 30%? Maybe much more if you're in marketing, coding or auditing – and even more if you develop "AI agents" that automate workflows without you or anyone else telling them what to do (more on this later).

It will also directly impact your leadership. You do not want to be the laggard in constant denial and you don't want to be a crazy AI fanatic either. You need insight, understanding and some balance. But if you have to tilt one way or the other, you need to tilt toward fanatic. AI will absolutely, positively change the way you do pretty much everything: how you think about AI is an inescapable priority. I realize this sounds like something a crazy AI fanatic would say, but you need to brace yourself for impact, which will come in expected and unexpected ways.

This book can help. It's not a complicated treatise on AI, or a theoretical look at how new technology can transform business models and processes. It's a series of conversations masquerading as chapters designed to help you understand AI, what it can do and what you should do about AI, ML and GenAI right now.

One assumption you should reject immediately is that you have a lot of time to think this through, perhaps even as much time as it took cars to totally replace horse and buggies, or about a quarter of a century. This time displacement will be incredibly fast. There won't be anywhere near as much time as there was during past industrial or digital revolutions because this one is moving at warp speed, is pervasive and in some cases existential. Some industries will be disrupted in every sense of the word – in just three-to-five years. In fact, it's already begun. Look at medical imaging, robotic manufacturing, financial services, legal research, auditing, marketing and coding, among more than a few processes that have already yielded to AI – and remember that this is just the first inning. Bullish on AI? Absolutely – and you should be too. Don't try to hide from this one. It will find you.

Here's a Q&A session about how you should think about AI. Let's use "marketing" as the example.

# What Is Machine Learning and Generative AI?

Here's how Gemini – a popular chatbot like Claude and ChatGPT – answered the question (with some help from me):

> With **machine learning**, instead of programming with specific instructions, you provide a lot of data. The computer then figures out patterns and relationships within that data, and uses those patterns to make predictions or decisions … like for image recognition (where) you show a computer thousands of pictures of cats, it can learn to recognize cats in new pictures … or language translation (where) a computer can learn to translate text from one language to another by studying millions of translated documents.

**Generative AI – on the other hand –** can generate **new** content like text, images, music or code. It's like having a creative assistant that can help you brainstorm ideas or produce something entirely original ... it also works by analyzing vast amounts of data and learning patterns. Then it uses that knowledge to create something new that's similar to what it's seen before, but also different and original.

## What's So Special About AI?

AI has the capability to automate more tasks than you can count, which means it can help you save lots of money. It's also a strategic technology that can make you more competitive – and very rich. Applications can be "taught" and can "learn" how to generate new content, video, code and images. AI is as special as the Internet was 25 years ago. Perhaps more importantly, AI is now a filter through which you should pass business problems of all shapes and sizes. This is a new best practice that forces problems to visit AI before they visit any other emerging technology. AI is also a consistent moving target which makes it special in another way. Capabilities today pale in comparison to capabilities tomorrow. For example, just a few years ago no one was talking about agentic AI.[1] Now AI agents (see below) are automating complex workflows everywhere.

## How Should – For Example – Marketing Processes and Business Models Be "Matched" with AI's Capabilities?

Marketing processes are straightforward and include at least market research, product development, advertising, social media marketing, sales, customer service, brand management and public relations. What you need to do is decompose these processes into subprocesses that can be matched to what AI can potentially do. You then need to identify the capabilities of ML and GenAI and match the two columns. For example, "advertising" consists of commercials, print ads and online everything. Can AI perform these tasks? Yes, it can.

## What Should You Be Doing About AI Right Now?

You should immediately develop a Task Force (comprised of hotshot "individual contributors") which should launch a competitor analysis, assess in-house talent and begin the marketing (or other) functions, activities, processes and subprocesses AI matching process to identify appropriate demonstration pilots. You should also find resources to assess the contributions AI can make. You need a team and a budget: this is not the time to ask your Chief Financial Official (CFO) how much you should spend on AI because you know what the answer will be. If you cheap out, you will lose out. Open the coffers. It's an investment opportunity you cannot afford to miss.

## Can You Just Ignore AI for a Few Years While It All Settles Out?

Again, only at your own competitive risk. AI is moving at a pace we've not seen before, so tracking progress is required. There's no evidence that delay is a smart strategy. You do not want to be the executive that sat on the fence as your competitors exploited AI. Your investors and Board of Directors will be very unhappy if you sit on your hands. This is not the time to tell them you're "looking at it." This is the time you tell them you already have an AI investment strategy.

## How Should You Manage the Inevitable Elimination of Jobs?

You should begin the process by communicating to the team that several things are happening. The first is the assumption that AI will impact the marketing (or other) profession in ways yet to be fully defined – but without question very significantly. You should communicate your expectation that the company will be able to save money and make money with AI. The message is that the company will immediately begin to start matching marketing (or other) functions, activities, processes and subprocesses to ML and GenAI. You should also communicate that there's every reason to believe that the number of employees at the company will shrink over time, *as it will with all service companies that sell concepts, words, images, video and advice.* Finally, you should communicate that there's no precise timeline for any of this – except the decision to start matching and piloting today has already been made. Will this shot across the bow get their attention? You bet it will. Some employees will leave the company as fast as they can. Some will seek jobs at companies less committed to AI, some will just wait and see if AI's for real – and some will look at how AI can improve what they do and how AI can help the company save money and make money. These are the keepers.

# How Are Your Competitors Using AI?

You need to understand how your direct and indirect competitors are using AI. You should pay particular attention to "new entrants" into the marketing (or other) area. Historically, most technology-enabled disruption comes from new companies – not your traditional competitors. Make sure you look over your shoulder – not at the same faces you see every year at industry conferences – but for companies committed to disrupting your company and your industry. Do you know who they are?

Track the investments venture capitalists are making in AI marketing (and AI generally). These investments reveal where AI will be in five years. Spend some time in the media sphere where AI is the topic of choice – like every day. While I'm not a huge fan of strategic consultants (I like operational ones a whole lot more), this may be the time you hire a few so-called thought leaders and AI gurus to wow you about where all this might land. If ever there was a time to think outside the box, this is it.

# Do You Have the Right People?

Since AI is relatively new and since your longer-term employees were trained in an era when ML and GenAI were in their applied infancy (if they existed at all), you likely do not have the right team to assess how AI can impact your company or your industry. You will need some newer professionals to do your assessments (and pilots), or – as suggested above – some consultants you can hire *short term* to assess the technology. Make sure these consultants are forbidden to implement their usual land-and-expand playbook. They have one job to do for you: assess-and-exit.

# How Should You Measure the Outcomes of AI Demonstration Prototypes?

Standard metrics for evaluating pilot applications should *eventually* be used, such as return on investment (ROI), key performance indicators (KPIs) and objectives and key results (OKRs) that measure cost savings, revenue generation, scalability, customer satisfaction and the like. *But if this is all new to you, traditional metrics should be relaxed.* What you need is a green light to do some more demonstration prototypes, not a direct link to immediate cost management or revenue generation. Make sure you don't insist that AI solve all of your operational or strategic problems right out of the gate. These are phase I demonstration prototypes designed to get to phase II. Ultimately, this is about alignment with your company's operational and strategic objectives, and your willingness to accept AI as transformational. But if you don't have shared operational and strategic objectives, your AI pilots will be hard to measure. If you don't have shared strategic objectives you need to develop them *fast*, if you expect to leverage AI in any meaningful ways.

## Who Should Lead These Efforts?

A well-respected, well-funded senior executive surrounded by individual contributors – not a large team – organized in a small Task Force. This is not the kind of project you give to a lower-level manager. This is not the kind of project you give to a well-known jerk or your friend because you're worried about the outcome. You need a business-technology leader who's widely respected primarily for his or her accomplishments, not relationships. I realize this recommendation is maybe not the one you want to hear. It's natural to want to surround yourself with friends who you believe you can trust. But not all of your friends are smart, dedicated or have the leadership qualities you need for this project. Yes, this is a big one, perhaps the biggest one you will ever launch. Pick the right professional for the job. Look to proven "individual contributors" to get the job done.

## Bonus Question: Who Are Your Friends?

You need to rethink your work friends. We all have them. The ones we like a lot, the ones we don't like as much, and the ones we think are smart – maybe smarter than they actually are. We also have trusted consultants – some of which we've turned to for advice for years, and maybe some new ones we've invited into the inner circle and even under the cone of silence. If we still have offices, there are friends' offices we routinely visit to just commiserate about the world, the company, your clients, fellow employees, your families, who knows what – the friends we lunch with, the friends we drink with, our coffee friends.

Why all this discussion about your friends? You're the boss, right? You don't need that many friends! You have most of the answers anyway, which is why you're the boss. Sure, you want to hear what others have to say (and read books like this), but at the end of the day – unless you're the world's only perfect "servant-leader," you believe you know what to do – which is precisely why you're paid the big bucks.

But you need some new friends these days. New lifelong friends with strange names that you may have just met. Friends like Claude, Chat, Grok, Manus, Llama, Perplexity, Copilot, Gemini and DeepSeek and a bunch of others who desperately want to be your friends, who have all been invited into this book's discussion. It's time you widened your circle of work friends. Maybe even some personal ones. It's time you started talking directly to Claude, Gemini, ChatGPT, Llama, Perplexity, Copilot, Grok, Manus and DeepSeek, and stay open to adding more friends into your circle of trust. You should also play with their friends and the tools they use to help you save money and make money. So stay tuned for some consultations with these new friends – who are also my friends. As you will see, I ask them for ideas, suggestions and "lists" – they're really good at making lists – throughout the book. Since they're as human-like as humans can be, I always acknowledge them by name: I don't want to offend them (who knows how they might react). Remember, they're not your servants, they're your friends. As such, this book is a living case study of how AI can make you more productive. Just ask Claude (or Gemini, ChatGPT, Llama, Perplexity, Copilot, Grok, Manus or DeepSeek). They will tell you what they can do to help.

## NEXT?

Ten questions (plus a bonus one) and ten answers (plus a bonus one).

Now it's time for more conversations about AI, which are intended to get you up to speed on AI, ML and GenAI. The hope is that you become "AI comfortable" in many ways, including launching a steady stream of demonstration prototypes to help your company explore what AI can and cannot do.

## NOTE

1   The distinction between "AI agents" and "agentic AI" is important. AI agents are software systems designed to perform specific tasks and pursue goals on behalf of users. They exhibit a degree of autonomy, reasoning, planning and memory. They're often built upon large language models and can process various types of information (text, voice, etc.). Agentic AI, on the other hand, is a broader concept that refers to AI systems designed to act with significant autonomy, often with limited or no human supervision. It's not just about executing tasks, but about perceiving, reasoning, planning, acting and continuously learning from its environment to achieve complex goals. The terms are sometimes used interchangeably here though the distinctions are always appreciated.

# PART I

# Executive Perspectives

# The Surprising Lack of Intelligence About Artificial Intelligence[1]

# 1

## ABSTRACT

*Despite the pervasive hype surrounding artificial intelligence (AI), machine learning and generative AI, a significant chasm exists between executive perception and practical understanding. This chapter presents the stark reality: while CEOs, CIOs and CTOs overwhelmingly acknowledge AI's importance, their actions reveal a profound lack of intelligence or appreciation of AI initiatives. Survey data highlights alarming levels of unpreparedness, insufficient funding and a late-stage adoption mentality across numerous organizations. This disconnect is juxtaposed with the aggressive pursuit of AI solutions by technology giants who recognize the immense financial opportunities. The chapter delves into the inevitable displacement of well-educated professionals across diverse industries. While the potential for cost savings and profit generation is clear, the critical question of how to manage this unprecedented workforce transition remains largely unaddressed.*

DOI:10.1201/9781003652748-2

There's a lack of intelligence, understanding and appreciation for artificial intelligence – even now! When surveyed, too many CEOs, CIOs and CTOs describe their relationship with artificial intelligence (AI) in some strange ways.

For example, only 20% of them define "AI" initiatives as high priority, and over 47% define them as insufficient or unknown. Only 25% adequately fund their AI initiatives and 37% believe they do "sometimes." When asked about where their AI initiatives appeared on the technology adoption curve, 53% describe themselves as "late majority," "laggards" or completely "unprepared" for AI. When asked specifically about generative AI (GenAI) – ChatGPT, Gemini, etc. – 23% said they have "explored the potential and risks of generative AI," but 77% said they had only looked at GenAI briefly or not at all![2]

Other surveys report the same "unreadiness." The Qlik/IDC survey (2025) measured a significant gap between ambition and execution: 89% of organizations have revamped data strategies for GenAI, but only 26% have deployed solutions at scale, and only 12% of organizations feel ready for agentic AI. The Cisco AI Readiness Index (2024) indicated that while the urgency to adopt AI is rising, overall readiness is falling! Only 21% of organizations have the necessary GPU infrastructure, and only 31% claim their talent is "highly ready" to leverage AI.

Given all of the hype around AI, machine learning and GenAI, how are these results even possible?

On the other end of the adoption curve, those who develop and sell AI solutions understand the financial implications. Amazon, IBM, Google, Microsoft, Meta, Apple, Intel and Nvidia – among many others – are racing to sell vitamin pills and pain relievers – smart applications that can make money and save money. You are waiting to deploy applications that will save you time, effort and money – *especially money you now spend on humans*. You see AI as a cost manager *and* a profit center – at least that's the hope.

But how should you prepare for the inevitable?

For perhaps the first time, you know that AI will displace *well-educated professionals* in the financial service, consulting, transportation, healthcare and manufacturing industries, and just about any industry that uses people to solve problems. Lots of us talk about the industries most likely to be impacted by AI, but very few talk about the small number of humans who create the technology, how the technology will inevitably become just another appliance or how the transition to machines will be managed. We also seldom talk about timing. When will displacement occur? How widespread will it be? How should you prepare?

What happens when displacement occurs? Hardly any of the AI gurus describe specific displacement management plans. This is the scary part of the story (not AI hostages or AI instigated Armageddon). How many industries and companies will know how – *or even want* – to manage displacement?

Corporate HR departments will explode with complaints and lawsuits and collapse under the weight of the exit packages they'll be forced to approve. Young *and* aging factory workers – and accountants, lawyers and doctors – will forget their purpose. Politicians will stare into the technology headlights – again – frozen by their own confusion and vested interests. Executives and shareholders will squeal with profitable delight. Universities will adjust their curricula or rapidly lose customers. Pain will pervade the corridors (but not the boardrooms) of the hard *and* soft industrial worlds, though this time the corridors will be wider and prettier than they've been in past displacement revolutions (because knowledge workers work in prettier places).

This is the part of the story that deserves more the attention, though very few analysts talk about what happens after displacement occurs. What happens to the lawyers, accountants, medical diagnosticians, manufacturers, supply chain managers and customer service representatives when they're displaced? Where will they go? What will they do? Let's call the question posed by Xavier Mesnard (2016) of the *World Economic Forum*:

> *The risk we are facing in the near future is mass unemployment for some categories of workers, combined with lack of skills in other categories – and the political and social implications of such imbalances.*

At a time when we cannot agree about healthcare, taxes, war, climate change or even evolution, there will be endless debates about what's actually happening and who's to blame, instead of what should be done to reeducate, retrain and redeploy displaced humans.

Since corporations will largely benefit from displacement (in the same way they benefited from cheaper global labor markets), governments may be expected to intervene. But given how clueless government already is about AI, and how slowly it moves even when it's informed and committed, the prospects for effective displacement management are dismal. It may be that we're focusing on the wrong problem – with the wrong problem-solvers.

You probably only have 3–5 years to figure all this out, which is a problem given the current level of intelligence about AI. There's a lot of education and analysis necessary to minimize displacement damage and optimize another round of digital transformation. The backdrop is complicated by a variety of other competing priorities. The first is always awareness.

*At the same time, everyone should see AI, machine learning and GenAI as one of the greatest business opportunities in decades both for those who create AI platforms and tools and those who want to deploy them for competitive advantage, which we do here in* How Executives Should Think About AI.

*We all have a lot to learn.*

*You have a lot to do.*

# NOTES

1   "AI" is used throughout the book to refer to AI, machine learning (ML) and generative AI (GenAI).

2   The data was collected by The Cutter Consortium, an Arthur D. Little (ADL) company in 2023–2024. The survey was developed by Stephen J. Andriole and Noah P. Barsky. Participants included CEOs, CIOs, CFOs, CTOs, SVP, EVPs and Senior IT Management: over 70% of the respondents were senior. The majority of the respondents were from North America (54%); Europe was second (24%). The industries that responded the most were financial services (15%) and computer consulting (13%). Beyond that, there was representation across many verticals split almost evenly. Forty percent of the companies have revenue of $1–50M and over 20% have revenue over $50M. Thirty percent have revenue over $1B. Eight percent have revenue over $50B.

# Why AI Is
# So Special

# 2

---

## ABSTRACT

---

*This chapter provides a pragmatic, urgency-driven introduction to the critical role of artificial intelligence (AI), specifically machine learning (ML) and generative AI (GenAI). It emphasizes the need for immediate executive action to understand and implement AI strategies, highlighting its transformative potential across all industries. It cautions against underestimating AI's impact, stressing its power to disrupt existing business models and displace knowledge workers at an unprecedented pace. The chapter proposes a practical approach, advocating for the formation of Task Forces, competitor analysis and pilot programs to assess AI capabilities. It also addresses the critical aspects of managing job displacement, securing necessary talent and objectively measuring AI pilot outcomes. The core message is clear: AI is the most significant technology in a generation that all executives must understand.*

There are lots of technologies that attract attention – and money. We're on-and-off obsessed with blockchain, cryptocurrency, the Internet-of-Everything (IOE), big data analytics, cybersecurity, 3D printing and drones. We're excited about virtual and augmented reality. We love talking about driverless cars, ships and planes. We can't wait for the next "G," and while we're worried about social media and privacy, we're still addicted to our ever-more-powerful smartphones. We buy everything online. We're attached to wearables. But there's one technology you really need to understand: AI. While there are other families in the disruptive digital technology world, this is the one you cannot treat as just another emerging technology, no matter how seductive the others appear to be.

# "SPECIAL" IS NO LONGER RELATIVE

AI is special because it's more than one technology. In fact, it's a family of technologies. Second, AI is special because its application potential is so wide. Next, AI is special because it learns and sometimes even self-replicates. AI is also special because it's improving faster than any technology we've ever seen before. It literally makes itself obsolete about every six months. Finally, AI is everywhere: who's not looking at in AI? There's a bona fide arms race underway among corporate and national players, which shows no signs of slowing anytime soon. *In short, AI is a phenomenon, and while many of your contemporaries will tell you that they've seen it all before, that technologies come and go and our natural reaction to all new technologies is to overhype them, you need to see AI differently.* Despite what the Gartner Group – a premier technology research organization – might tell you, AI will not slide into the "trough of disillusionment," whatever that actually is.

Remember that AI includes at least machine learning, deep learning, image recognition, robotic process automation, generative AI, large language models, generative pretrained transformers (GPTs), natural language processing, computer vision, agentic AI, robotics, neural networks and pattern recognition, among other methods, tools and techniques. Yes, it's a big technology.

# WHAT AI CAN DO

AI will profoundly impact healthcare, transportation, accounting, finance, manufacturing, customer service, aviation, education, sales, marketing, law, entertainment, media, security and war. No industry, function or process is safe from the impact AI will have in the short run and especially over the next five-to-seven years. Remember that AI will integrate across business and technology architectures, databases and applications.

The timing – as always with the adoption of emerging technologies – is debatable, and the changes will not all be good. Note the ease with which disinformation can be created and disseminated by intelligent creators, and how easy it is for smart bots to service personal and professional confirmation biases intended to manipulate thinking and behavior. At the same time, good bots will make much of our personal and professional lives more productive, freeing us to pursue other, so-called higher-level activities. Will AI eliminate jobs? Of course, and this time the elimination will include so-called knowledge workers as well as the traditional manufacturing jobs we associate with robotics. Much of this capability will arrive simultaneously across whole industries, such as how the automotive industry will utilize robotic AI to manufacture driverless cars and then manage their movement across cities and towns across the world. Similarly, healthcare will be impacted by monitoring, diagnoses and treatment. AI will not kill us, but it will augment and replace many of us in the workplace. Again, it's a question of *when*, not *if*, impact will occur.

Regardless of how bullish or bearish you are about displacement, it's safe to say that tens of millions of jobs – *and knowledge-based careers* – will be impacted – and in many cases eliminated by AI. Some of these jobs include (Saleem, 2023):

- Entry-level programming, data analysis and web development roles
- Entry-level writing and proofreading roles
- Translation jobs
- Entry-level graphic design jobs
- Fast food order taking jobs
- Accounting
- Postal service clerical jobs
- Data entry jobs
- Bank teller jobs
- Administrative support jobs
- Legal roles
- Packers/packagers
- Entry-level HR roles
- Mathematical technician roles
- Insurance claims and policy processing jobs
- Telemarketing

Here's a list from Leitch (2023):

- Tax preparers
- Locomotive engineers
- Parking enforcement workers
- Warehouse stockers
- Watch repair technicians
- Cashiers
- Meter readers
- Mail sorters
- Data entry keyers

- Casino dealers
- Prepress technicians
- Taxi drivers
- Engine and machine assemblers
- Fast food workers
- Referees
- Telemarketers
- Farm workers
- Translators
- Librarians
- Computer programmers
- Proofreaders
- Textile workers
- Toll booth operators
- Legal secretaries
- Dispatchers

But should other professionals be on the list? Is there some line analysts won't cross about what AI can and cannot do? Are there classes of professionals immune to algorithms? Here are some of the seldom discussed professionals also in the crosshairs of AI:

- Strategists
- HR managers and executives
- Writers (of all kinds)
- Project managers
- Program management officers
- Social media analysts
- Competitive intelligence officers
- Radiologists
- Student advisors
- Disinformation "professionals"
- Teachers (including professors, trainers and tutors)
- Newscasters
- Directors and managers
- Artists
- Musicians
- Architects

Do any of these people work for you?
Are *you* on the list?

# PROCESS MODELING AND MINING

Step one is the modeling of your current and aspirational processes informed generously by the potential of AI and predictions about the evolution of your industry. Elaborate process models should be developed, tested, simulated and inventoried to inform your AI demonstration pilot agenda. The simplest way to build this agenda is to identify the processes most amenable to AI and simulate the impact intelligent systems might have on the costs and benefits of the target processes. Robust simulations should rank-order the processes that should be piloted with new technologies.

The first step is to develop a process inventory that describes how you do business – literally how your company works – and then perform process mining to identify the processes that cost you the most time and money. Once this is done you can match the "bad" processes with AI – processes that can be improved, automated or eliminated with AI, machine learning and generative AI. In other words, you need targets to improve, automate or kill. The more the better.

Unless you already have an inventory, you should proceed with process modeling and mining. If you have an inventory, you should begin to "match" the problems with potential AI solutions. As you read through this book, the matching process will become clearer. You will see where AI can help. You will identify some of the AI tools that will improve, automate or eliminate the targeted processes.

# THINK PARTNERS

Along the way to your AI strategy, you should aggressively pursue corporate partnerships. You need enabling partners that, for example, provide AI development and application platforms (which will come from their cloud providers in most cases). University partnerships are also valuable. You should befriend AI start-ups. Many companies scan the start-up terrain for acquisition targets. You should too.

You're planning a moonshot. Hopefully, you've already found the money to get started and you're developing a perspective that "works" in your company, at least one that greenlights some pilots and prototypes. But as I said in the Introduction, make sure you deputize some new digital partners as well. You already know their names.

# Why Classical IT Needs Some AI Jazz

# 3

## ABSTRACT

*Every company is a technology company, but many executives still ignore the strategic imperative of AI. This shift marks a transition from "classical" IT to "jazz" improvisation, where AI acts as the maestro. Operational technology is now commoditized, leaving strategic AI as a differentiator. AI is not just another technology, but a fundamental infrastructure and applications platform, reshaping business processes and models. Companies must move beyond incremental adaptation, embracing radical change and leveraging AI to drive innovation. This requires a commitment to understanding and mastering AI, analogous to learning a complex musical instrument. Without this commitment, companies risk being left behind, stuck in the "classical" era of complacency.*

It's all-digital now, from how you operate your company, to how you design your products and services, to how you attack the marketplace. None of this is new. It's been true since the turn of the century, though there are still executives – *I hope not you* – who refuse to believe they actually run technology companies, which every company is and will be forever. No? Remove all of the technology from your company and see what's left.

Way too many executives still believe their companies can be run as a set of distributed functions shared with a variety of outside vendors. Imagine how many vendors there often are, and how challenging it is to manage

DOI:10.1201/9781003652748-4

multiple contracts. Not to mention the number of interdependencies across your providers. Just remember that one single configuration file update can crash half the world (Bishop and Kharpal, 2024). AI can declutter and reinvent this mess. New ways of thinking about classical and jazzy technology can help.

## AI JAZZ

AI is the strategic change that analysts, vendors, consultants, CIOs, CTOs and CEOs *still* often fail to see. AI is one of those pivots – like what we saw with the Internet – that you see, or you don't, the kind of pivots that allowed companies like Uber, Airbnb, VRBO, PayPal and Stripe into the game as major players in vertical industries and essential infrastructure providers of all things transactional.

Do you see it?

OpenAI and Nvidia are there now, along with hybrid technology vendors like IBM, Microsoft, Meta and Google, all trying to pivot before their customers pivot somewhere else. Yes, it's on – and you're in the middle of it, whether you fully realize it or not.

Note that the lane the Internet opened has opened for AI – and then AI opened its own lane. But this one is far wider and impactful than the Internet ever was. In fact, while the Internet was an enabling technology that led to all sorts of new business models, AI is both an infrastructure *and* an applications platform that rides on the Internet *and* its own large language models (and everyday algorithms like regression, and more complex ones like convolutional neural networks).

## THE SOUNDS OF MUSIC

Imagine the journey a musician might take from classical to jazz. Once upon a time, technology – when done well – was classical music, the same way finance, accounting and HR – when done well – were classical. You've probably thought about "IT" (information technology) that way for years. You compared it to other business functions and processes, which in the 20th century was appropriate. But while accounting, finance and HR have obviously changed, they're still more classical than jazzy. Technology, on the other hand, morphed into something that bears no resemblance to its 20th century self. It moved from the back office to the front office, took over the building, connected the world and then stood up and looked around for more things to do. The classical-to-jazz journey converts old classical fans to jazz fans – the full and forever integration of business and technology.

Here's what your friend Gemini thinks:

*Classical music prioritizes the composer's written score and structured performance, while jazz emphasizes improvisation and the performer's spontaneous creation. Essentially, classical music is about reproducing a pre-existing work, and jazz is about creating a new one in real-time.*

The switch from classical to jazz assumes that business-technology is a concert with very different music than the concerts you've probably attended. Digital technology – powered by AI – is the latest, and ongoing, improvisation. As more and more operational technology is commoditized in the cloud, leverage lies in the strategic application of emerging technology to current and future business processes and models prioritized by how much they impact current and future products, services and markets. AI is the maestro.

Business processes and whole business models must change, not just adapt: incrementalism-by-default is the enemy, in spite of how much safe political capital it generates. You must improve them, automate them, reinvent them – or just kill them altogether. But what do you replace them with? Which technologies make this happen? Which are relevant to your primary and adjacent markets – and markets you cannot even see today? Do you know how all this works – together? Or how it will work next year? AI will change just about everything. While we just entered the normal doubts about the return on investment (ROI) around AI, be careful not to be seduced away from the unlimited potential of machine learning and generative AI. It's all jazz now. You have no choice but to adapt even if you've been classically trained, which most companies have been over decades. It's not like learning how to play golf left-handed. It's about learning a whole new sport whose moves and rules bear no resemblance to the sports you play. It's like learning how to play the French horn in a month, not the bongos you've already outsourced. AI's the French horn. It's complicated, but capable of some of the most beautiful music you've ever heard.

# COMMITMENT

Let's assume you're given no choice, that you're told you must learn how to read music and then play the French horn. Where do you start? You first need to assess how musical your team is. You then need to hire some good instructors. You need some instruments. But most of all you need commitment. If there's no commitment, you're going to have to somehow motivate your team to appreciate the complexities of AI jazz. Without commitment you'll be stuck with the same old beautiful classical music you've been listening to for decades. Beautiful, quiet and complacent – and that's how it ends. Think about it.

# How Machine Learning and Generative AI Change Business

# 4

## ABSTRACT

*This chapter describes the capabilities of machine learning and generative AI through direct interaction with ChatGPT and other chatbots. The question "why are machine learning and generative AI so important?" elicits a comprehensive overview of its potential to revolutionize product design, medical research and marketing, among other activities. The question "is generative AI just another technology fad?" prompts a discussion regarding its transformative potential versus hype. The distinction between machine learning and generative AI are also examined, highlighting their differing foci: machine learning on predictive tasks, and generative AI on content creation. Finally, the importance of generative AI is emphasized, citing its potential for creativity, efficiency, personalization, insight generation and novel applications. The chapter demonstrates the value of chatbots like ChatGPT, Claude and Gemini as accessible tools for understanding complex AI concepts.*

Let's ask ChatGPT (and some other chatbots) some questions and see what kinds of answers we get. Let's start with "why is machine learning so

DOI:10.1201/9781003652748-5

important?" Note that this is a joint effort: I worked with Chat to answer this and other questions:

- Machine learning (ML) is crucial for companies because it enables smarter decision-making, enhances efficiency and provides a competitive edge. By analyzing vast amounts of data, ML helps businesses make accurate predictions, such as sales forecasts, customer preferences and market trends. It also automates repetitive tasks, reducing costs and minimizing human error in areas like customer service, data entry and fraud detection. Additionally, ML enhances customer experience by personalizing recommendations, as seen with how Netflix suggests movies, Amazon recommends products and Spotify develops playlists.
- Security and fraud detection are also improved with ML, as it can identify unusual patterns that indicate potential threats, helping industries like banking and finance. In manufacturing, ML supports predictive maintenance, helping companies anticipate equipment failures before they occur, thus reducing downtime and repair costs.
- It also optimizes operations and logistics by improving supply chain management, inventory forecasting and delivery routes. Amazon and FedEx are good examples of companies that leverage ML for improved logistics.
- Marketing strategies are also improved by ML, which enables companies to target the right audience with personalized ads and content, increasing conversion rates. Ultimately, ML provides a significant competitive advantage, allowing companies to make faster, more cost-effective decisions. Those who adopt ML early gain insights that others might miss, positioning themselves ahead in their respective industries.

What about generative AI (GenAI)? "Why is it so important?"

GenAI is a type of artificial intelligence (AI) that's able to generate new, original content based on a set of input parameters – AKA "prompts." GenAI actually has the potential to revolutionize a number of fields, including:

- **Creative Industries**: GenAI can create original works of art, music and literature. This enables the creation of new content much faster than is possible with humans alone.
- **Product Design**: GenAI can design new products based on a set of desired characteristics. This can lead to the creation of novel and innovative products that might not have been possible with traditional design methods.

- **Medical Research**: GenAI can generate new hypotheses and ideas for medical research.
- **Marketing and Advertising**: GenAI can create new marketing and advertising campaigns based on a set of desired outcomes.

# MACHINE LEARNING VERSUS GENERATIVE AI

## "What's the Difference Between Machine Learning and Generative AI?"

ML is a method of training AI systems to perform tasks by exposing them to data and allowing them to learn from it. It involves training a model on a dataset and then using the trained model to make predictions or decisions based on new inputs. ML can be "supervised," in which the model is trained with labeled data and the desired output is provided, or "unsupervised," in which the model is not given any labeled data and must find patterns and relationships in the data on its own.

GenAI is focused on generating new content, such as text, images or audio. It does this by learning the patterns and characteristics of a particular type of data, and then using that knowledge to create new, similar examples. GenAI can be trained using various ML techniques, such as neural networks or probabilistic models.

One key difference between ML and GenAI is that the latter is specifically designed to generate new content, whereas ML can be used for a wide range of tasks, including prediction, classification and optimization.

# WHY SHOULD YOU CARE?

## "Why Should You Care About Generative AI?"

There are several reasons:

- **Creativity**: GenAI has the potential to create new, original content in a way that is difficult or impossible for humans to do. This can be particularly useful in art, music and literature, where creativity is literally key.

- **Efficiency**: GenAI can potentially generate large amounts of content quickly and efficiently, which can be useful in situations where a large volume of content is needed, such as in marketing or content creation.
- **Personalization**: GenAI can be used to create customized content for individual users, based on their preferences and characteristics. This could be used to create personalized advertisements, recommendations and other types of content.
- **Novel Applications**: GenAI has the potential to enable new and innovative applications that were previously impossible. For example, it could be used to create personalized education materials and to design and optimize new products and processes.

ChatGPT, Claude and Gemini – among other chatbots (AKA "friends") – can help you understand AI. All you have to do is ask. As discussed, if these bots aren't part of your life, they should be. They're pretty smart about how AI can impact your business – even your specific company (not to mention your competitors).

So I just had to ask Claude – one of your new work friends – about corporate executives (like you?) who don't spend much time with them:

*Executives who aren't spending time with AI chatbots are making a strategic mistake. This isn't just about staying informed; it's about competitive survival. AI tools like chatbots represent a fundamental shift in how businesses can operate, and executives who remain hands-off are essentially flying blind ... executives who don't engage directly with these technologies ... cannot properly evaluate AI investment decisions, misjudge both the potential and limitations of the technology, are likely making uninformed assumptions about how competitors are using (and) risk being blindsided by AI-driven market disruptions.*

*It's comparable to executives in the 1990s who dismissed email and the Internet as passing trends or delegated all digital understanding to IT departments. Those companies often found themselves scrambling to catch up years later.*

I could not have said it better.

# How AI Actually Works

# 5

## ABSTRACT

*This chapter addresses the need for executives to develop a functional understanding of artificial intelligence (AI), machine learning (ML) and generative AI (GenAI) to effectively navigate investment decisions, strategic planning and technology trajectories. The chapter argues for an "executive understanding" that encompasses key terminology, the breadth of potential applications and the significance of emerging trends in the field, such as the pursuit of "reasoning," energy consumption challenges and evolving computational architectures – all considered at a solutions level rather than deep engineering specifics. Through a glossary and some examples, the chapter demystifies AI.*

You need to know how AI, machine learning (ML) and generative AI (GenAI) actually work. Let's start with a short glossary that I wrote with the help of some bots. But before we get into it, it's important to make the case for the "executive understanding" of AI, ML and GenAI. You must understand AI at a level that will enable you to understand investment decisions, strategies and trajectories. You must understand the terminology, you must understand the range of potential applications, you must be able to interpret the significance of new companies like DeepSeek, Manus and others, the march toward AI "reasoning," the challenges around energy consumption and even computational architecture – again, not at the engineering level, but at the solutions level.

Yes, you're an "executive," but you cannot be a leader that asks someone how the Internet works, which is a question I actually received from the

DOI:10.1201/9781003652748-6

Managing General Partner of a huge private equity venture capital fund expected to invest in Internet companies in the late 1990s. I was asked what the Internet was, how it works and where it came from – no kidding. You don't want to be the executive who asks those kinds of questions about AI. Said a little differently, you never want to be the executive who's dismissed among the troops as an AIdiot.

# AN AI GLOSSARY

I asked ChatGPT to help me develop an AI glossary, which we did together (actually, most of it is mine). Nevertheless, you should welcome this kind of assistance whenever it's available:

**AI** includes lots of pieces. First, whenever someone mentions "AI," it's important to make sure that "AI" includes at least ML and GenAI, and all of the other parts of the field that attempts to solve problems the way humans do. The field includes ML, deep learning, computer vision, image recognition, GenAI, large language models (LLMs), generative pre-trained transformers (GPTs), natural language processing (NLP), agentic AI, robotics, neural networks, among other methods, tools and techniques. Summarize it this way: AI enables machines to "sense," "think" and then "act" just the way humans do. It does so more or less efficiently as humans do today, but will get better and better at "sensing," "thinking" and "acting" over time – much faster than humans improve over time.

**ML** is just that. Humans teach a machine how to perform tasks by just showing the machine how the tasks are performed. For example, the task of approving or rejecting a loan is a very straightforward process full of steps humans take all the time. The steps can be modeled and defined, such as looking at an individual's credit score and past loan history. Machines can be taught to take these steps and find the data necessary to enable the credit-checking task. In this example, machines (with "algorithms") can be taught how to mimic human behavior so that humans no longer need to be involved in the loan approval process. ML enables computers to learn from data and improve performance without explicit programming. ML identifies patterns and makes decisions (or predictions) based on input data. It helps in automation, predictions and decision-making. There are several kinds of ML including "supervised learning," where a model is trained on a "labeled" dataset, meaning each input data point has a corresponding correct output or "label." The algorithm learns to map inputs to outputs. Next is "unsupervised learning," where the model is trained on "unlabeled" data, meaning there are no predefined output labels. The algorithm's goal is to discover hidden patterns, structures or relationships within the data on its own. The third is "reinforcement learning," where an algorithm learns by interacting with an environment where it receives "rewards" for desired actions and "penalties" for undesirable actions. "Semi-supervised learning" combines elements of both supervised and unsupervised learning. It's used when you have a small amount of labeled data and a large amount of unlabeled data. The model uses the labeled data to learn initial patterns and then uses the unlabeled data to refine its understanding or generate new labels. The last is "self-supervised learning," which creates its own "labels" from the input data itself, often by setting up a "pretext task." The model then learns to solve this pretext task, and in doing so, it learns useful representations of the data that can be applied to downstream tasks.

**Algorithms** are "rules" that a computer follows to solve a problem or perform a computation. Algorithms define how data is processed and transformed into outputs. They're step-by-step instructions that tell a computer how to solve a problem or perform a task. They're "recipes" that guide how computers process information and solve problems, used in everything from search engines to fraud detection. Some of them are straightforward – like multiple regression – and some are more complicated – like neural networks (see below). Some help you solve simple problems – like whether or not to approve a loan – and some solve much more complicated problems – like how self-driving cars avoid hitting pedestrians.

**NLP** focuses on the interaction between computers and human language. NLP enables machines to understand, interpret, generate and manipulate text or speech, as seen in chatbots and language translation tools. **NLP** understands and works with human language, like chatbots or voice assistants that enable computers to understand, generate and interact using human language, powering tools like chatbots and voice assistants. NLP includes natural language understanding and natural language generation.

**Computer Vision** enables machines to interpret and analyze visual information from the world, such as images or videos. It's used in facial recognition, object detection, medical imaging and autonomous vehicles. **Computer vision** enables computers to "see" and make sense of images and videos, like facial recognition or self-driving cars.

**Image Recognition** enables computers to identify and classify objects, people or patterns in images. It's used in security (facial recognition), retail (self-checkout), healthcare (medical imaging) and manufacturing (quality control). Computer vision and image recognition work together across applications to solve a variety of problems – such as how a robot knows when a tomato is ripe or not ripe for picking.

**Robotics** involves the design, construction, operation and programming of robots. Robotics integrates AI, computer vision, image recognition and ML to create autonomous or semiautonomous machines. It involves the design and programming of robots to perform tasks, from factory work to home assistants. **Robotics** use of AI-powered machines to perform physical tasks, from warehouse automation to robotic surgery.

**GenAI** generates new content, such as text, images, music and videos, by learning from existing data. Examples include ChatGPT for text generation and Stable Diffusion for image creation (though chatbots can also generate images). GenAI creates new things, like writing text, making images, composing music and transforming industries like marketing, content creation and design.

**Neural Networks** are computational models – algorithms – inspired by the human brain, consisting of layers of interconnected nodes (neurons). They're the foundation of deep learning and are used in tasks like image recognition, speech processing and language modeling. They're designed like a simplified version of the human brain, used to recognize patterns and make predictions. They are the "go to" algorithms for all things complex.

**GPTs** are LLMs based on the transformer architecture, pretrained on vast text datasets to generate human-like text. Examples include OpenAI's ChatGPT, Anthropic's Claude and Google's Gemini. They're smart AI models that can understand and generate text and other kinds of output. They're models that understand and generate human-like text, revolutionizing customer service, content creation and automation. Think of them like interfaces to huge amounts of data – like all of the data on the Internet.

**Custom GPTs** are tailored versions of GPT models that are fine-tuned or configured for specific tasks, industries or users, allowing for personalized responses or domain-specific expertise. **Custom GPTs** are versions of GPTs that are fine-tuned for specific needs, like customer service or medical advice. They're like specialized consultants that cut to the chase. They know a lot about some things but not that much about everything.

**AI Agents** are software systems designed to perform specific tasks or pursue goals on behalf of users. They exhibit a degree of autonomy, reasoning, planning and memory. They're often built upon LLMs and can process various types of information (text, voice, etc.). They're used in applications like virtual assistants, automated trading systems and even aspects of self-driving cars.

**Agentic AI** is a broader concept that refers to AI systems designed to act with significant autonomy and adaptive decision-making, often with limited human or no supervision. It's not just about executing tasks, but about perceiving, reasoning, planning, acting and continuously learning from its environment to achieve complex goals.

**LLMs** are trained on massive datasets to understand and generate human-like text. They power applications like chatbots, content creation tools and code assistants. They're trained on massive amounts of text to generate human-like writing and conversations. They enable conversations with Gemini, ChatGPT, Claude and all the rest. LLMs work by predicting the next word in a sequence based on patterns learned from massive amounts of text data.

**Small Language Models (SLMs)** are similar to LLMs but trained on smaller datasets, making them more efficient, faster and suitable for specific tasks with lower computational demands. They're "lighter" versions of LLMs that are faster and work better for smaller tasks. Many companies are defaulting to SLMs to keep their data private.

**GANs (Generative Adversarial Networks)** are models – algorithms – that consist of two neural networks, a generator and a discriminator, that compete against each other to create realistic data (e.g., synthetic images, videos or text). GANs create realistic images, videos or texts by having two AI models compete with each other to generate the best possible outcomes.

**Prompt Engineering** is like giving really good instructions to a super smart but sometimes not-so-intuitive assistant (the AI) to get the exact results you want. Bad prompt engineering sounds like "draw a picture." Good prompt engineering sounds like "draw a photorealistic image of a golden retriever puppy playing fetch on a sunny beach at sunset." Prompt engineering is about crafting your requests (prompts) with enough detail and clarity so AI understands exactly what you want it to generate, whether it's text, images, code or something else. It's about learning how to "talk" to the AI effectively to unlock its full potential.

# HOW IT ALL WORKS

Let's look at how AI actually works with a few examples. Let's first look at how ML works.

# Machine Learning

Let's look at an example of how ML solves a problem: picking ripe tomatoes. How does it do that?

The first thing it does is "see" tomatoes which has been "trained" to identify ripe versus unripe tomatoes. It does this with computer vision. Once it "sees" a ripe tomato – defined by image recognition – the robot picks it and places it into a bin. How was it "trained"? Well, it was shown hundreds of pictures of ripe and unripe tomatoes and was "taught" to recognize one versus the other. It's actually a pretty simple example of supervised learning.

Let's describe the process in a little more detail with Claude's help. Here's how a robot picks a tomato, step by step:

- **Detection:** Using computer vision through cameras and sensors, the robot scans the tomato plant and identifies ripe tomatoes based on color, size and shape. The robot's vision system is trained on thousands of images of tomatoes in various stages of ripeness, lighting conditions and positions. These datasets include labeled images indicating which tomatoes are ripe and ready for picking.
- **Analysis**: The robot processes the image data to determine the exact location of each tomato in 3D space and evaluates which tomatoes are ready for harvesting based on ripeness criteria. Algorithms refined through real-world performance in actual growing conditions. Before field deployment, robots often train in virtual environments where they can practice identifying and picking virtual tomatoes. This helps refine algorithms without risking real crops. During initial development, human operators often validate the robot's decisions, providing feedback when it incorrectly identifies ripeness or makes picking errors. Some advanced systems use reinforcement learning where the robot receives "rewards" for successful picks and "penalties" for damaged fruit or missed targets.
- **Planning**: The robot calculates a path to reach the target tomato without damaging surrounding plants, stems or other tomatoes. The robot arm moves toward the identified tomato, carefully navigating through the plant foliage. As it gets closer, the robot uses more precise sensors (possibly including tactile feedback) to make final positioning adjustments.
- **Grasping**: depending on the design, the robot either uses a specialized soft gripper that conforms to the tomato's shape, employs vacuum suction cups to gently hold the fruit or uses a scissor-like cutting mechanism combined with a catching system.

- **Detachment**: The robot either applies gentle twisting and pulling motion to separate the tomato from its stem, or uses small blades or scissors to cut the stem while holding the fruit or employs a combination of both techniques. The robot carefully moves the picked tomato away from the plant without squeezing too hard or dropping it. The harvested tomato is transferred to a collection bin, conveyor belt or sorting system.
- **Reset**: The robot arm returns to position and begins the process again with the next identified ripe tomato.

As you can see, the process uses lots of AI – computer vision, image recognition, ML, robotics – to achieve a specific outcome. The same kinds of steps are taken to approve or deny a loan. A (ML) system "sees" data – like credit history and income – and "decides" – based on lots and lots of good/bad loan experiences – if the loan should be approved or denied. The accuracy of this "decision" can be tested over time until it's success/failure ratio equals – and then surpasses – the "decisions" loan officers make every day. (So do we still need loan officers?)

Here are a few other examples of ML:

**Predictive Maintenance:** ML algorithms analyze data from sensors on equipment (e.g., machinery in a factory, engines in vehicles, HVAC systems) to predict when failures are likely to occur.

**Customer Churn Prediction:** ML models analyze customer data (e.g., purchase history, website activity, engagement metrics, customer service interactions) to identify customers who are at high risk of leaving.

**Fraud Detection:** ML algorithms learn patterns of fraudulent behavior from historical transaction data (e.g., credit card transactions, insurance claims, online activity) and can identify anomalous activities in real-time.

**Personalized Marketing and Recommendations:** ML models analyze customer behavior and preferences to deliver personalized marketing messages, product recommendations and offers.

**Supply Chain Optimization:** ML algorithms analyze vast amounts of supply chain data (e.g., demand forecasts, inventory levels, transportation costs, supplier performance) to optimize inventory management, predict potential disruptions and improve logistics.

**NLP for Customer Service and Insights:** A subfield of ML that enables computers to understand and process human language. Applications include chatbots, sentiment analysis of customer feedback and automated analysis of customer service interactions.

# Generative AI

How about a look at GenAI? Here's how Zewe (2023) explains GenAI:

*Generative AI can be thought of as a machine-learning model that is trained to create new data, rather than making a prediction about a specific dataset. A generative AI system is one that learns to generate more objects that look like the data it was trained on.*

Think of GenAI this way:

**Learning from Data:** AI is first "trained" on massive amounts of data. For image generation, this would be millions of images of various things. For music, it would be countless songs across different genres. For video, it would be a huge library of video footage. During this training, the AI identifies the statistical relationships between different elements (e.g., the shape of a cat's ear, the typical melodies in a pop song, how light and shadow work in a video).

**Understanding Your Request**: When you give the AI a prompt, like "a cat wearing a tiny hat," it analyzes your request to understand the key elements you're looking for.

**Generating Something New:** Based on its training and your prompt, the AI starts to create something entirely new.

**For an Image:** It might start with random noise and then iteratively refine it, adding shapes, colors and textures that align with its understanding of cats and hats, aiming for a photorealistic style.

**For a Song:** It might generate a sequence of notes, rhythms and instrumental sounds that fit the style you implied (or explicitly requested), creating a unique melody and arrangement.

**For a Video:** It could generate a sequence of frames, depicting movement and visual elements consistent with your prompt, perhaps even adding simulated camera movements.

**Here's an example of how *new images* can be created.** Let's say an AI tool has been trained on many pictures of dogs and many pictures of beaches. If you ask it to create "a golden retriever running on a sunny beach," it will:

**Understand "Golden Retriever":** It knows the typical colors, shapes and features of a golden retriever.

**Understand "Sunny Beach":** It knows about sand, water, sky and the bright lighting associated with a sunny day.

**Combine:** It will then generate a new image that combines these elements in a plausible way, creating a picture of a golden retriever running on sand with water and a bright sky in the background. This image wouldn't be a copy of any specific image it was trained on, but a novel creation based on its learned understanding of dogs and beaches.

GenAI learns the "rules of the game" from existing data and then uses those rules to create entirely new content that follows those rules. GenAI is like a chef who has learned the fundamental techniques of cooking and can then create new and original recipes.

How about video? Imagine you want a short video of "a cat playing with a ball of yarn in a sunlit room." GenAI starts with a prompt: "A cat playing with a ball of yarn in a sunlit room." It then "understands" the objects, setting and action. It then selects or generates 3D models/2D sprites of the cat and yarn. Then it selects or generates a suitable room environment, animates the cat's movements to simulate playing, defines camera angles and movements and then renders each frame and sequences them into a video.

In effect, GenAI for video acts like a virtual director, animator and cinematographer. It uses its knowledge of physics, animal behavior and film-making techniques to create a new video based on your instructions. The challenge lies in coordinating all the elements – objects, motion, camera – over time to produce a coherent and visually appealing sequence.

Prompt engineering acts as the *instruction manual* or the *creative brief* you give to the GenAI artist. The quality and clarity of the prompt directly influence the quality of the output.

How about computer programming? How has that changed? In the old days – like five years ago – programmers actually wrote code from scratch in a number of programming languages, like Python, Java and even C. But now?

In essence, the role of a programmer is evolving from being primarily a "code writer" to more of an "orchestrator" or "guide" of the AI in the development process. This involves steps that every programmer – or non-programmer – takes:

- **Prompt Engineering**: Effectively communicating with AI tools using clear and concise instructions to get the desired output.
- **Reviewing and Validating AI-Generated Code**: Ensuring the correctness, security and efficiency of the code produced by AI.
- **Understanding the Limitations of AI**: Recognizing when AI-generated code might be incorrect, biased or require human intervention.
- **Focusing on the "Why" and "What"**: Spending more time on understanding the problem domain, defining requirements and designing the overall solution.

- **Leveraging AI for Innovation**: using AI tools to explore new possibilities and accelerate the creation of innovative software solutions.

So do you still need all those programmers you keep on staff? Or all those programmers sitting in countries far, far away? No, you don't. In fact, it's time to completely rethink your programming sourcing strategy.

## Machine Learning Versus Generative AI

Let's revisit this. Think of ML as primarily focused on understanding and predicting patterns in existing data. It's about learning from the past to make informed decisions or forecasts about the future. GenAI goes a step further. It learns from existing data, but its primary goal is to create *new, original content* that resembles the data it was trained on.

ML and GenAI serve different purposes. ML helps us understand and predict, enabling better decision-making and automation based on existing data. GenAI empowers us to create new possibilities, opening doors for innovation in content creation, design and even problem-solving by generating novel solutions.

OK, now it's time to play with some AI.

# Time to Play AI

# 6

## ABSTRACT

*This chapter emphasizes the importance of direct executive engagement with AI tools. It argues that executives must actively "play" with AI to appreciate its capabilities and limitations, particularly in the context of their daily responsibilities. The chapter outlines key executive activities, such as decision-making, planning, communication and risk management, and curates a "playlist" of AI tools relevant to each area. The chapter also highlights some "special tools" like NotebookLM, avatars and AI agents. It details how these tools can revolutionize information management, communication and workflow automation, offering practical examples of their potential impact on executive funtions and organizational processes.*

It's time to play with AI. While I realize that you usually have people do things for you, there's no substitute for some hands-on experience with your new friends. When someone says, "Claude thinks we should do it this way," or Gemini thinks "it's a bad idea," or "we can just convert the meeting into a podcast," you need to understand how this happens. The same is true about tools like NotebookLM, avatars and AI agents. These should not be abstractions. They should not be tools you think you understand. You should be able to hold a conversation about what they can do.

You should know how these tools apply to your professional lives, the lives of your employees and how they impact your company. You do not need to understand the mathematics of algorithms that power everything, but you do need to understand that there are "algos" driving machine learning and generative AI processes, such as who gets a loan and how new music is created. So the best way to understand what AI can and cannot do is to play with the tools.

DOI:10.1201/9781003652748-7

# EXECUTIVE ACTIVITIES

So what *do* you do all day?

There's actually a lot of research about what executives do all day – including what *you* do all day. You make lots of decisions. You plan. You manage risk. You communicate with email, meetings, Town Halls, newsletters, briefings and brief encounters in the hallways or long ones on Zoom. You perform market and financial analyses, you work with customers, clients and vendors, you build your brand, you hire and fire people, you find/remove office space, you buy companies, you sell companies, you invest in technology, you hire and fire consultants, you track projects, you manage stakeholders and investors and you never get enough sleep.

Can AI help with any of these activities? Do you ever just play with some of the tools to see what they can do? Maybe not – but you should.

# PLAYLIST

Here's a breakdown of what you do and the AI tools that can help you perform the tasks more efficiently. It's loosely organized, but you get the idea – which is to play with them to get a feel for how they work and what they can and cannot do.

Let's start with a list of the "chatbots" that you may already probably use, such as:

- OpenAI's ChatGPT
- Microsoft's Copilot
- Google's Gemini
- Anthropic's Claude

Here's a list of chatbots that you probably use less, if at all:

- Perplexity AI
- Butterfly Effect's Manus AI
- DeepSeek AI's DeepSeek
- ByteDance's Doubao
- Meta's AI
- xAI's Grok

While you probably have only used a few of these, they all essentially do the same thing: enable "conversations" that generate "new" content based on enormous data bases trained into large language models. If you haven't played with one or more of these bots, it's way past time you did.

Let's look at a few of the things you do and the AI tools that might help. Claude and I found some tools organized around the things you do – though I'm not sure everything on the list makes sense (mostly Claude's stuff for sure). You will notice that many of the things you do, and the suggested tools, are probably beyond what you do, though some executives may do them all day. Regardless, it's an interesting attempt to match activities and tools. It's more to make a point than to make you learn some tools you won't ever need, but you should know about them. So here's the list:

Market Analyses and Forecasting

- Tableau with Einstein Discovery (for predictive analytics and data visualization)
- Power BI with AI Insights (similar to Tableau, from Microsoft)
- Trendlyne (for financial data, market trends and analysis)
- CB Insights (for venture capital, startups and emerging technology trends)

Risk Assessment and Mitigation

- FRISS (for AI-powered fraud detection in insurance)
- RiskQuant (for quantitative risk management)

Communication and Information Management

- ChatGPT (from OpenAI; for general text generation, summaries and more)
- Gemini (from Google; similar to ChatGPT, Google's large language model)
- Jasper (for marketing copy and content creation)
- Otter.ai (for meeting transcription and summaries)
- Zoom with AI Companion (for meeting summaries, and other AI-assisted meeting functions)
- Microsoft Teams Premium (for intelligent meeting recaps and tasks)
- AI-Enhanced Email Management (Gmail/Outlook with AI plugins)

Operational Efficiency and Productivity

- UiPath (RPA platform with AI capabilities)
- Automation Anywhere (RPA platform with AI features)

- Blue Prism (RPA platform with AI integrations)
- Google Analytics 4 (GA4; for website and app analytics with AI insights)
- Salesforce Einstein Analytics (for CRM data analysis)
- AI-Enhanced Calendar and Scheduling (Google Calendar with smart features)

Customer Relationships and Business Development

- Salesforce Einstein (for AI-powered CRM insights and automation)
- HubSpot with AI features (for marketing and sales automation)
- AI for Lead Generation and Sales Forecasting

Image Generation

- Adobe Photoshop (industry standard for professional image editing and creation)
- Canva (user-friendly graphic design platform with templates and drag-and-drop functionality)
- GIMP (free, open-source alternative to Photoshop)
- Procreate (popular digital painting app for iPad)
- Midjourney (AI image generator creating images from text descriptions)
- DALL-E (OpenAI's text-to-image AI system)
- Stable Diffusion (open-source AI image generation model)
- Affinity Photo (professional photo editing software with one-time purchase)
- Pixlr (browser-based photo editor with free and premium options)
- Clip Studio Paint (digital art software popular with illustrators and comic artists)

Video Generation

- Adobe Premiere Pro (professional video editing software)
- Final Cut Pro (advanced video editing software for Mac users)
- DaVinci Resolve (professional-grade video editor with strong color correction tools)
- iMovie (free, user-friendly video editor for Apple devices)
- Filmora (accessible video editor with effects and templates)
- Runway (AI-powered video editing and generation platform)
- Descript (video editor that allows editing video by editing text)
- Capcut (popular mobile video editing app)
- OBS Studio (free, open-source software for video recording and live streaming)

- After Effects (motion graphics and visual effects software)
- Sora (OpenAI's text-to-video AI model that can generate realistic and creative video content from text descriptions)

Many of these tools are easy to use, but many are way too difficult for non-technologists to even try. Again, I am in no way suggesting that you – as an executive – undertake a long learning process to master some tools that might make your professional life more bearable. In fact, you should not spend time learning most of these tools. You have much more important things to do. But there *are* some tools you and your team can play with to improve your professional life. This is the (processes/AI tools) matching process I discuss throughout the book.

If you look at the list, there are many areas of little or no interest to you. But if you look more closely you will see a category that you will probably find valuable, and that's the one on "Communication & Information Management." These tools can become your playmates. At the very least, you might play with the presentation tools like Gamma, Presentations.ai and Beautiful.ai. If your job ever requires you to create presentations, these tools are much better than the traditional PowerPoint app that you may have used for years. There are others, including Google Slides, Pitch and Microsoft Copilot Pro. The point? There are tools that will help you do what you do better and faster. You might also try tools like Otter.ai that record meetings and enable you to analyze and summarize what was discussed.

Seven Favorites
Let's pick some favorites:

1. For text-based questions: ChatGPT
2. For image generation: DALL-E
3. For simple workflows: Zapier
4. For avatars: Synthesia
5. For business productivity: Notion AI
6. For analytics: MonkeyLearn
7. For agentic AI: AgentGPT

# PROMPT ENGINEERING

As discussed several times, almost all of the tools require some skills in "prompt engineering," which (SCC, 2024)

*Refers to the practice of designing and refining inputs – known as "prompts" – to guide AI systems in generating relevant and effective responses ... by understanding how to phrase questions, commands, or statements clearly and strategically, you can get more meaningful results from these AI systems.*

There's more:

*Think of prompt engineering like communicating with a very smart assistant. If you provide vague or poorly structured instructions, the assistant will struggle to deliver the results you're looking for. On the other hand, a well-crafted prompt can unlock highly valuable insights, saving time, improving efficiency, and boosting productivity.*

Some organizations – like JPMorganChase – are actually requiring their employees to become skilled prompt engineers.

You should prompt the chatbots just to learn what they can do. You need to get comfortable conversing with them all. You should ask different chatbots the same things to understand how they might answer you differently – which they will. You should ask them to evaluate everything even what the other bots are saying about each other! Iteration is important. If you don't get the response you believe you should get, ask again – and again. You should prompt the tools designed to generate images and videos, like Midjourney, DALL-E and Sora.

Prompt engineering is how you talk with all of these tools and applications. Over time, these prompts will become easy conversations, which is what they need to be even for executives. You can speak to them the same way I'm speaking to you right now. This is a skill you should master. You should master the "text-to ___ " process, like text-to-video, text-to-images, text-to-coding, text-to-music and text-to-building custom GPTs, LLMs and even AI agents. It turns out that "talking" to these tools enables "new" – new music, content, analyses, images, videos, code, art – you name it.

# SOME SPECIAL TOOLS

There are a few tools you should try. One is NotebookLM, which is a Google application that manages data in some extraordinary ways. Google initially described it this way (Martin and Johnson, 2023):

*NotebookLM is ... use(s) the power and promise of language models paired with your existing content to gain critical insights, faster. Think of it as a virtual research assistant that can summarize facts, explain complex ideas, and brainstorm new connections – all based on the sources you select.*

Gemini explains what you can do with the tool:

- **Summarize Information**: NotebookLM can summarize complex documents, generate key topics and ask questions to help you understand the material.
- **Answer Questions**: You can ask NotebookLM questions about the documents you've uploaded. For example, you can ask it to create a glossary of key terms or summarize interactions between people.
- **Create Personalized Guides**: NotebookLM can generate a personalized guide based on your sources.
- **Create Podcasts**: NotebookLM can generate realistic podcasts from documents.
- **Create Study Guides**: NotebookLM can create study guides with short-answer questions and a glossary of important terms.
- **Create Briefings**: NotebookLM can create briefings from your sources.
- **Analyze Sources**: NotebookLM can analyze sources, such as email marketing funnels.
- **Brainstorm Connections**: NotebookLM can help you brainstorm new connections based on the sources you select.

As Gemini explains, "you can use NotebookLM with a variety of sources, including Google Docs, PDFs, Text files, Google Slides, Website URLs, Audio files, and YouTube links."

*NotebookLM is as flexible with words as Excel is with numbers.* In fact, the two applications work equally well at different ends of the analytical continuum. NotebookLM is designed to enable insights, concepts, ideas, brainstorming and collaboration in ways that are not dissimilar from how Excel enables insights, concepts, ideas, brainstorming and collaboration. One tool uses words and one uses numbers.

You should play with NotebookLM. It's free, and if you like to "read" with podcasts, it's terrific.

You should also play with avatars – especially ones of yourself (with your cloned voice). While it may sound crazy, within a few short years, for example, colleges and universities will begin to use avatars to teach especially online courses. The AACSB (Association to Advance Collegiate Schools of Business), which stamps "approval" on business schools, has already looked at the possibilities (Hiskey, 2024):

*How would business education change if all instructors were assisted by avatars – virtual doppelgängers that look and sound just like them? More broadly, how would student learning be affected if every classroom included an artificial intelligence (AI) component?*

Synthesia is one of the tools educators are using (and the tool my students are using for all sorts of projects) to create virtual professors – and the one you should play with. Note that these avatars are not in any way "cartoonish." If a professor – *or you!* – wants to make a presentation, an avatar can be created to deliver the presentation (in any language).

You can create an avatar of yourself. If you've ever recorded a video of yourself, you know that some of them are better than others. Avatars can help. Virtual executives can present material with other executives to communicate important corporate messages. You might think about how we want to leverage these capabilities. You need to be aware of how these tools can help you communicate with your teams and investors.

What about AI agents? Everyone should understand what AI agents are, how they work and how they impact business processes and models. So let's start with the basics. AI agents perceive their environment, make decisions and act to achieve specific goals. They're used in applications like virtual assistants, automated trading systems and self-driving cars. AI agents can make decisions and complete tasks, like virtual assistants or self-driving cars. They perform tasks autonomously, such as handling customer inquiries, managing workflows or optimizing logistics. They automate workflows – what you do all day – without intervention: they work all by themselves once you tell them what to do – once. But what does this really mean?

AI agents – and the broader field of "agentic AI" – are the most important AI capability we've seen to date. Here's how we see it:

- Imagine your most capable human assistant, but one that can learn, adapt and work tirelessly across multiple complex tasks without needing constant instruction. That's the essence of agentic AI.
- Think of traditional AI like a sophisticated calculator or a very specific tool. You give it a precise input, and it gives you a precise output. It's good for repetitive tasks or analyzing large amounts of data in a predefined way. It's like giving your assistant precise instructions and expecting the instructions to be perfectly followed. But imagine giving the assistant a goal, not just a list of tasks. Just imagine what you could ask agents to do.

Here's how AI agents work:

- **Agents Have Goals**: You tell the agent what you want to achieve, not just the steps to take. For example, you could tell an agent to "increase customer satisfaction by proactively addressing their issues."

- **Agents Can Figure Out How To Get There**: Instead of you telling it exactly what to do at every stage, it can analyze the situation, come up with a plan and decide on the best course of action. It can use various tools and information at its disposal.
- **They Can Learn and Adapt**: If its initial approach isn't working, agents can analyze why and adjust their strategy. They get smarter over time as they gain experience.
- **Agents Can Work Independently**: Once given a goal, agents can often operate without constant human oversight, freeing up your team's time for more strategic initiatives.

Why is this so important?

- **Solving Complex Problems**: Agents can tackle intricate issues that are too dynamic or involve too many variables for traditional automation. Think of optimizing complex supply chains or personalizing customer journeys at scale.
- **Boosting Efficiency and Productivity**: Agents can automate entire processes that currently require multiple people and handoffs, leading to significant time and cost savings.
- **Creating New Opportunities**: Agents can analyze data and identify patterns that humans might miss, leading to new insights, product ideas or ways to better serve your customers.
- **Improving Customer Experience**: By understanding individual needs and proactively addressing issues, agents can create more personalized and satisfying customer interactions.

Think of agentic AI in practical terms:

- Instead of a system that just answers customer service questions based on a script, agents could proactively identify customers who might be having issues, reach out with solutions and even resolve the problem without human intervention.
- Instead of manually analyzing market trends, AI agents could continuously monitor data, identify emerging opportunities or risks and even suggest strategic adjustments.

The key takeaway is that AI agents move beyond simple automation to intelligent problem-solving and goal achievement. They have the potential to handle more complex, dynamic and strategic tasks, leading to significant improvements in efficiency, innovation and customer satisfaction.

While there are still considerations around ethics and implementation, understanding the fundamental shift toward more autonomous and intelligent

AI agents is important for you to leverage AI, machine learning and generative AI.

So there you have it. Agents can automate you, your team and your company. They're extremely important to understand. They're one of the most powerful capabilities of AI. You must understand what they are and how they work. You should also understand how to match your business processes with agents.

"Agentic AI" is where lots of the action is today and will likely be over the next few years. Agents will also reduce the need for prompt engineering in some significant ways. There's also a larger question of just how smart these agents can become and how many processes they might automate – on their own. Agentic AI can potentially disrupt all kinds of business processes, business models and whole business strategies. You need to watch this area very, very closely. If I were you, I'd request a monthly briefing from my team on just how impactful agentic AI is becoming, who's using agents to their advantage and how you might launch some agentic AI pilots so you can develop some demonstration prototypes – which is a perfect segue to Part II of this book.

# PART II

# Executive Actions

# AIQ Tests

# 7

## ABSTRACT

*This chapter addresses the challenge of AI talent scarcity within organizations and emphasizes the critical role of "mindset" in effectively leveraging AI. It contrasts linear and nonlinear thinking, arguing that while traditional linear approaches can optimize well-defined processes with machine learning, the transformative potential of generative AI lies in its capacity for non-linear problem-solving and innovation. The chapter highlights how generative AI can unlock hidden value and drive creativity by navigating complex, interconnected data beyond the limitations of linear models. The chapter introduces a series of "AIQ Tests" designed to gauge knowledge across fundamental concepts, practical applications, data and tool awareness, strategic thinking and prompt engineering. It concludes with an executive education program outline aimed at deepening the understanding of AI, machine learning and generative AI.*

You probably don't have enough talent at your company to explore how AI can improve, automate or replace the business processes that save you money or make you money. You're not alone. Most companies are starved for AI talent – a condition that's likely to persist for a long time until higher education produces enough AI expertise to close this business-technology gap. Playing "catch up" is always hard. Upskilling is also challenging but may be all you can do.

DOI:10.1201/9781003652748-9

# LINEAR VERSUS NONLINEAR THINKING

The first challenge is how you and your team think about AI at a systems level. Think about it. The relationship between problems and AI is not linear – the way you and you just about all problem-solvers think about it (MindManager, 2025):

> *Linear thinking ... follows a known step-by-step progression similar to a straight line. Linear thinkers view a problem as a process ... that follows a sequence of connected series, ultimately leading to a solution ... thoughts flow in a straightforward, logical way, and progress in a stepwise fashion.*

Nonlinear thinking is different (Charles, 2009):

> *Non-linear thinking is less constrictive – letting the creative side of you run rampant because of its inherent lack of structure. It's kind of like letting a puppy run wild on a walk up a mountain – anything of interest will be thoroughly investigated.*

Note that there are variations on these definitions, including lateral thinking, systems thinking, design thinking and fragmented thinking – among others – but for our (and Gemini's) purposes here, the simple linear versus nonlinear distinction is fine.

Lots of *well-bounded, linear processes* can be performed better, faster and cheaper with simple machine learning (ML) tools. Regression + supervised learning is AI's little secret: they're everywhere – and they work. But the game-changing opportunities lie with generative AI (GenAI) and its potential for nonlinear thinking and problem-solving. The leap from supervised to unsupervised learning ("thinking") is one way to think about the potential. But it goes way beyond simple applications.

# GENAI IS NONLINEAR

According to Gemini – and in response to my prompt – "are the applications of generative AI more linear or nonlinear?" – here's how to think about the potential:

The applications of GenAI are driven by *non-linear* models.

Here's why:

**Real-World Data Has Complex Relationships:** GenAI deals with things like images, text and music. The connections between features in this data (e.g., colors in an image, words in a sentence) are intricate and often context-dependent. Linear models struggle to capture these complexities.

**Neural Networks Are the Workhorse:** GenAI relies on neural networks, which are inspired by the human brain. These networks use nonlinear activation functions to process information and learn patterns. This allows them to handle the nuances of real-world data.

**Examples Highlight Nonlinearity:** Consider generating a new song. A linear model might just string random notes together. GenAI, however, can learn the complex relationships between melody, harmony and rhythm to create something that sounds musical.

I then asked Gemini: "what are some linear business problems that AI solves pretty well?"

Linear business problems are a perfect fit for AI's strength in optimization. Here are some examples of how AI tackles linear problems in the business world:

- Inventory Management
- Pricing Optimization
- Route Planning
- Marketing Campaign Optimization
- Financial Ratio Analysis

But what about return on investment (ROI)? What if a company wanted to know which flavor of AI in which it should invest? I asked: "how do I get the best return on my GenAI investments? Linear or nonlinear business problems?"

GenAI's power lies in tackling *non-linear* business problems. Here's why focusing on nonlinear problems offers a higher potential return:

**Unlocking Hidden Value:** Many complex business challenges involve intricate relationships that linear models can't capture. GenAI, with its nonlinear approach, can identify subtle patterns and connections in data, leading to innovative solutions and uncovering hidden value.

**Boosting Creativity and Innovation:** GenAI can generate new ideas, automate creative tasks and personalize experiences. This can lead to entirely new product concepts, marketing strategies or customer service approaches that wouldn't be possible with linear thinking.

**Augmenting Human Expertise:** GenAI can analyze vast amounts of data and identify patterns that humans might miss. This can empower human employees to make better decisions, solve problems more creatively and focus on higher-level strategic tasks.

However, this doesn't mean you should ignore linear problems entirely.
Here's a *combined approach* for maximizing your return:

**Identify Bottlenecks:** Start by using AI for tasks well-suited to linear models, like optimizing pricing strategies or managing inventory levels. This frees up resources and provides a solid foundation for further investment.

**Focus on Nonlinear Opportunities:** Then, explore how GenAI can address complex business challenges with nonlinear elements. This could involve personalizing customer experiences, developing new content formats or automating design tasks.

**Prioritize Strategic Impact:** Align your GenAI investments with your overall business goals. Focus on areas where AI can create a significant competitive advantage or unlock new revenue streams.

By combining the efficiency of linear AI with the innovative power of GenAI, you can maximize your return on your AI investments and drive real business transformation.

You should prioritize non-linear thinking and investments. Entrepreneurs should especially think this way. Quoted in Cordovez (2016), Pascal Finette says it plainly:

*Linear thinking is the path to doom for new ventures. We're losing lots of opportunities in a world where linear thinking clashes with exponential trends.*

ML and GenAI offer enormous opportunities to save money and make money. In order to identify and optimize these opportunities, companies need to search and destroy embedded linear thinking. While this does not mean there's no payoff to linear problem-solving – which there clearly is – it means that in order fully leverage GenAI new approaches to "thinking" must be adopted. Inevitably this means jettisoning the old ways, which is perhaps why Marriott did not "invent" Airbnb or VRBO. Or why McDonald's did not invent Impossible Meat, or how to increase its appeal or lower its production costs instead of abandoning the whole McPlant initiative (Pointing, 2024). Or how Uber came to be? Or why autonomous agri-business is yielding great returns?

Is nonlinear thinking ultimately about innovation? Absolutely, but it's also about the marriage between innovation and GenAI. Prompt Gemini about "the relationship among innovation, generative AI and nonlinear thinking?" The answer is a playbook – which leads us back to how AI kills linear thinking. Think about it and how married your team is to linear solutions for which nonlinear ones are much better matches.

Once you get the team thinking in linear and nonlinear terms, there's an AI skills gap you have to address. Let's think about some "tests" you might give to your team before you measure just how much AI expertise you need.

# AIQ TESTS

There are lots of ways to test your and your team's AIQ. Let's start with some very basic questions:

1. What is AI, ML and GenAI?
2. What is the difference between AI, ML and GenAI?
3. Can you give an example of how AI is being used in your industry today?
4. What are some of the risks associated with using AI?
5. What are some of the opportunities AI presents to your company?

The chances are high that your and your team's knowledge of AI, ML and GenAI is not as wide or deep as it should be. As suggested, you may not think about AI in ways that optimize its nonlinear potential. You may even be underestimating AI's linear potential.

If all that's true, you should try to identify the knowledge gaps and then respond with the design of some executive education around AI, ML and GenAI.

Let's start with five measurement tests I developed with Gemini that will enable you and your team to measure how much they know abbot AI, ML and GenAI:

**AI Concepts and Terminology**
Questions:
What does "Machine Learning" primarily involve?

- Creating robots that mimic human behavior
- Enabling computers to learn from data without explicit programming
- Developing complex algorithms for data storage
- Building advanced hardware systems
- Define "Generative AI" in your own words.

Which of the following is an example of AI-powered automation?

- Sending an email
- Using a spreadsheet
- Automatically categorizing customer support tickets
- Creating a presentation

What is "bias" in AI, and why is it a concern?
What is a large language model?

## Practical AI Applications

Scenario: Your team is responsible for improving customer service response times. You have access to a large dataset of customer inquiries and support tickets.
Questions:

- Describe how you could use AI to analyze the customer inquiry dataset to identify common issues and improve response times?
- What AI-powered tools could you use to automate responses to frequently asked questions?
- How would you evaluate the effectiveness of the AI solutions you implement?
- How could you use a GenAI tool to help with creating customer service response templates?

## Data and Tool Awareness

How many of these tools are you familiar with?

- Natural language processing (NLP)
- Predictive analytics
- Robotic process automation (RPA)
- ChatGPT
- Data visualization

## Strategic AI Thinking

Questions:

- How do you envision AI transforming your department or the company in the next 3–5 years?
- What are some potential AI-driven innovations we could explore to gain a competitive advantage?
- What steps should we take to ensure our team is prepared for the changes brought by AI, including training and upskilling?
- How would you measure the ROI of an AI project in your department?

## Prompt Engineering

Questions:

- Create a prompt that will summarize a five-page document into a one-page executive summary.

- Create a prompt that will take a list of bullet points, and turn them into a formal email.
- Create a prompt that will take a customer service complaint, and generate three possible responses, that are different in tone.

You and your team should take these or some other tests. You can push the tests down through your organization to get a feel for your company's AIQ. But then what? You've already dipped your toes into how AI "works," played with the tools and engaged in some conversations with the chatbots. Now it's time – if you're willing – to go a little deeper. Here's an executive education program outline that might help you and your team understand AI, ML and GenAI a little better:

# AI, MACHINE LEARNING AND GENERATIVE AI

1. The Strategic Importance of AI
   - Module 1: Demystifying AI
   - Module 2: The Competitive Landscape of AI
   - Module 3: AI's Impact Across the Value Chain
   - Module 4: Ethical Considerations and Responsible AI Governance
2. GenAI and Strategic Implementation
   - Module 5: Unleashing Creativity and Automation with GenAI
   - Module 6: Formulating an Organization-Wide AI Strategy
   - Module 7: Building and Scaling AI Capabilities
   - Module 8: Measuring the Impact and ROI of AI Initiatives
3. The AI-Powered Future
   - Module 9: The Future of AI and Its Disruptive Potential
   - Module 10: Leading the AI Transformation: A Call-to-Action Program

This should be seen as a study guide – no more and no less. You can find some consultants or academics to help you learn a little more about AI, ML and GenAI. There are online courses everywhere. This knowledge should trickle down to your team, where you know just enough and your team knows a lot more.

# Find Some Individual AI Contributors

# 8

## ABSTRACT

*This chapter challenges the conventional reliance on teams for AI implementation, arguing that the current lack of widespread AI expertise necessitates a strategic focus on identifying and empowering "individual AI contributors." It critiques the inefficiencies often associated with team-based projects and argues that highly skilled individuals with deep business acumen and AI proficiency can be significantly more effective in applying generative AI tools. The chapter defines the unique value proposition of individual contributors – their deep expertise, focused autonomy, speed, agility and creative potential – and how these qualities are amplified by the capabilities of generative AI.*

Every executive on the planet has favorites – the "go-to" professionals they turn to every time there's important work to do. You do too. But there are problems with this de facto best practice. As discussed, it's likely that even your "go-to" buddies don't know enough about AI to get you to where you need to go.

Go-to professionals are sometimes "individual contributors." But what you need is a new kind of individual contributor – one that understands both your business *and* AI. These people are hard to find. They're also usually not part of the team you assemble to get AI right. That's right: your Task Force – which you absolutely need – is probably weaker than it should be. It should be

DOI:10.1201/9781003652748-10

comprised of "individual contributors" who you manage mostly lightly (while you manage their uniqueness, see below for more on this contradiction).

# TEAMS DON'T WORK

You know it, I know it, everyone knows it: teams don't work. There's a mountain of research that describes just how bad teams can be. Coutu (2009) reported on some interviews conducted with the organizational guru, Richard Hackman:

> *In the course of their discussion, he revealed just how bad people often are at teamwork ... his research shows (that) team members don't even agree on what the team is supposed to be doing.*

What about all the fuss around "project management"? Aren't all those expensive certifications supposed to make teams more effective? Your friend Gemini sums it up:

> Project teams often fail due to poor planning, inadequate communication, unclear objectives, unrealistic expectations, scope creep, limited resources, ineffective leadership, lack of risk management, and improper resource allocation, which can lead to confusion, delays, and missed deadlines among team members and stakeholders.

# FIND SOME INDIVIDUAL AI CONTRIBUTORS

You should consider how to find and use "individual contributors." Note that the term itself is sometimes pejorative, often describing employees who are difficult to manage or whose value is hard to measure, though Mark Zuckerberg famously said that "someone who is exceptional in their role is not just a little better than someone who is pretty good. They are 100 times better." He's right. So what *are* individual contributors (Hone, 2025)?

> *Individual contributors ... work independently and are accountable for their work. In addition, they are typically subject matter experts in their*

*area of work and possess specialized skills, knowledge, or experience that enable them to perform their tasks with high proficiency.*

Chat describes when to use them:

**When Deep Expertise Is Crucial**: Individual contributors often possess specialized skills and knowledge honed over years of experience. In situations requiring deep expertise, their focused approach can be invaluable.

**For Tasks Requiring High Focus and Autonomy:** Individual contributors thrive in environments where they can work independently, focusing deeply on tasks without the distractions of team dynamics.

**When Speed and Agility Are Paramount:** In fast-paced environments, individual contributors can often make decisions and execute tasks faster than teams, as they don't need to navigate group consensus.

**For Highly Creative or Innovative Tasks:** Individual contributors may excel in generating original ideas and solutions, as they aren't constrained by the need to align with a group.

Generative AI (GenAI) – the ability to quickly create new code, images, video, content, music etc. – and tools like NotebookLM and AI agents – are rocket fuel to individual contributors. While the same tools are of course available to teams of all shapes and sizes, there's a special role they can play in problem-solving. Individual contributors who can leverage GenAI can multiply their contributions. While teams can also leverage GenAI, individual contributors may be in a position to leverage the tools faster than teams. In fact, since teams will likely "fight" even about which tools to use (and how to use them), individual contributors can adopt and apply them faster and more effectively *simply because they're individual contributors!*

# MANAGE THEM LIGHTLY

Sometimes individual contributors are difficult to manage. Sometimes they believe they're the smartest people in the room – even when they're not (and especially when they are). Sometimes they're independent members of a team and sometimes they're truly independent. Sometimes they shadow teams. They should obviously have deep expertise, be highly focused, can act fast, can pivot and be creative. This means that individual contributors are uniquely talented, which by definition means there's never enough of them – assuming that you want to leverage individual contributors with or beyond teams. Should you grow them? Should you encourage them? Should you hire more of them? Since you can't grow them, you should encourage (and financially reward) them, and you should hire as many of them as you can find.

Managing individual contributors is a challenge not just for the reasons listed above, but also because you must manage them along with the other professionals also trying to assess, develop and apply AI solutions to an array of problems in your company – who might be sensitive to the attention that individual contributors receive. If you're committed to individual contributors – as I've been throughout my career – then you must manage some jealously and insecurity – and you must do it without remorse. Coddling has no role here. You need to discover how AI can make you more competitive. Anyone that gets in the way of that objective should be removed.

# Sourcing AI

# 9

## ABSTRACT

*Sourcing technology, particularly artificial intelligence (AI), presents a signifi-cant challenge for organizations. This chapter examines the critical decisions surrounding how companies can acquire the necessary AI capabilities at the right time and cost. It explores the range of technology sourcing options, from developing AI expertise in-house with existing teams, to partnering with external vendors through outsourcing, or adopting a hybrid co-sourcing approach. A key distinction between "AI brains" – the strategic thinking and vision behind AI adoption – and "AI brawn" – the practical development and deployment of AI solutions – is important. The chapter argues that while out-sourcing the latter can work, relinquishing control over AI strategy to external consultants carries considerable risks. Developing internal AI expertise is a fundamental core competency. The chapter also examines the crucial concept of AI adoption, framing it within the well-established technology adoption curve. It highlights the unique complexities and accelerated pace of AI development, urging companies to proactively position themselves as innovators or early adopters to maintain a competitive edge. The discussion extends to potential sourcing partners, ranging from agile gig workers and innovative startups to established vendors, while cautioning against defaulting to traditional, poten-tially slower, less specialized and more expensive large consultancies.*

Technology sourcing is always a challenge. Where do you get what you need when you need it for a price you're willing to pay? Let's look briefly at your options for technology sourcing – especially AI sourcing. You can insource technology with your existing team. You can outsource technology with trusted vendors, or you can co-source technology with both. The trick is to know when you should do what for AI. At the end of the day, since you likely don't have all

DOI:10.1201/9781003652748-11

of the AI expertise you need, you need to look elsewhere – at least until you get up to speed on AI, machine learning (ML) and generative AI (GenAI) *which you definitely should do!* Don't rely on outsiders to develop your AI strategy unless you want others to tell you how to use AI to run your company.

# AI BRAINS VERSUS AI BRAWN

There's a distinction between AI brains and AI brawn you should understand. Let's remember that many sourcing decisions are made without direct "executive" participation. Outsourcing AI "strategy," however, to consultants is always questionable, no matter how storied the reputation of the consultancy. The premise is that there's a range of activities that form an AI brains-to-brawn sourcing continuum which you should continuously assess. Outsourcing AI brains is dangerous; outsourcing AI brawn can make sense. You need to know which is which, and the sourcing options around brains versus brawn. You also need to know which work they need to perform themselves and which is safe to outsource. So what are we talking about? AI brains include strategic thinking about how and where AI can make your company more competitive. AI brawn includes the development of demonstration prototypes and deployments that result from successful pilots. If you need consultants to define your AI strategy there's a larger issue at your company and among your executive team. Outsourcing the drudge work to consultants is often the best and perhaps only way to use them.

Sourcing decisions around AI, machine learning and GenAI are as important as any sourcing decision you will ever make. As discussed in Part I, it's an area that you should understand at least at the applications level. At the same time, it's likely that many companies – maybe even yours – don't have the in-house expertise to actually optimize AI, machine learning or GenAI. So what should you do? Self-awareness is essential here.

# AI ADOPTION

The goal is effective AI technology adoption and the sourcing partners you need to make it happen. As discussed throughout this book, the applications of AI, ML and GenAI to business models and processes are endless. Companies must constantly examine AI, ML and GenAI methods, tools, techniques and platforms, including large language models (LLMs), generative pre-trained transformers (GPTs), agentic AI, proprietary LLMs, custom GPTs, prompt engineering, AI agents, natural language processing, computer vision and algorithms (especially neural networks), among other AI methods, tools and platforms.

According to Gemini, "technology adoption is the process of learning and using new technologies, and can involve individuals or organizations. It can also refer to the integration of new technologies into a business's operations and strategies." The well-known "technology adoption curve," worth describing again here, includes:

- **Innovators**: The first to adopt a new technology and are often the youngest, most social and have the highest financial resources
- **Early Adopters**: The second fastest group to adopt a new technology and are often younger, have a higher social status and have more financial resources
- **Early Majority**: Adopt a new technology after a varying amount of time and make up the largest group of users
- **Late Majority**: Another large group of users who adopt a new technology
- **Laggards**: The last group to adopt a new technology

The technology adoption curve can be applied directly to AI, ML and GenAI, but there's a twist: complexity, development speed and the breadth of AI's applied potential. There's not a lot of time to decide how you want to adopt AI, because its capabilities increase dramatically every year.

So where do you want to be along the AI adoption curve? Who do you want to be – an innovator, early adopter, member of the early majority crowd, a late adopter or a laggard? What kind of help do you need?

Let's kill the last three adoption categories right now. "AI" gives you two choices: innovate or adopt as early as possible – and your sourcing decisions should be consistent with where you want to be along the technology adoption curve and which sourcing partners you should engage.

Let's also not forget how addicted companies can be to processes, meetings, bureaucracies, task forces, committees, governance, politics, lawyers and really long product development cycles. Public companies find it difficult to move at all, which often gets them into trouble. They're often too risk averse. Mid-sized companies are schizophrenic: fast on Monday, painfully slow on Tuesday and paralyzed for the rest of the week. Start-ups are open to most anything. Gig workers pivot on a dime. They can adopt a new platform overnight – and immediately offer it to their clients. They can just as quickly discard a platform in which they've made only a minimal investment. So you have opportunities and constraints depending on who you are and how you decide to source – if you don't get in your own way.

# AI SOURCING STRATEGY

Remember the discussion about "individual contributor's" in the last chapter? Sourcing is from the same family. While you should find and reward individual contributors to develop your AI strategy, you should extend the concept to sourcing partners who exhibit the same kind of fast, directed behavior – at least until you get your AI team up to speed.

You should look to gig workers, start-ups and small businesses to help develop your AI sourcing strategy. You should also look at traditional sourcing partners but make sure they have the expertise to actually perform the AI work you need them to perform.

Medium-sized and large companies are dangerously slow to adopt technology for the reasons described above. So are their traditional consultants. Can big companies accelerate the AI, ML and GenAI adoption process? Maybe. It all depends on their C-Suites and the executives who live there. In addition to traditional and unconventional sourcing strategies, you should also keep your eyes open for aqui-hires of AI talent. As discussed, many companies often don't have the talent to pursue AI, ML and GenAI initiatives, so they need help. You can try to upskill your teams, but it's much faster and efficient to just acquire companies and people who understand the technology – if you can find (and afford) them.

The adoption of AI can be fast, slow or not at all. Gig workers can spend a month learning a platform like Synthesia and become capable of generating some incredibly creative solutions to a variety of problems. They can learn how to develop AI agents and custom GPTs. They can learn how to generate new code, music and images. *They can be incredibly effective sourcing partners.*

At the end of the day, this all depends on what you want to do. It also depends on how flexible you are about sourcing. My recommendation is that you consider all of your options and not automatically just call McKinsey, BCG, Bain, Accenture, PWC or Deloitte. There are sourcing partners out there that may know more, can move faster and are much less expensive than the usual sourcing suspects.

I must emphasize again how important in-house AI expertise is. Too many areas of expertise have been outsourced to any number of more than willing (and often not so able) consultants. In fact, over the years the use of consultants for all things digital has grown almost as fast as take-out food. This technology requires some depth. It's essential that your strategic thinking be directly influenced by AI. It's even more important that your operational and tactical investments extend from your AI strategy. Please don't punt this one. Make sure that your AI strategy is really yours.

# Demos All Day Long

# 10

## ABSTRACT

*The most effective way to convey complex ideas and secure buy-in is through tangible demonstrations. This chapter argues that demanding working prototypes for any AI initiative, whether internal or external, is not just advisable but required. These "Board Grade" demos serve as the ultimate executive summary, transforming abstract concepts into understandable and relatable solutions. By showcasing AI in a problem-solving context, prototypes can communicate AI's unique capabilities and its potential to address specific business challenges, invent novel business models and drive competitive advantage. The chapter emphasizes the importance of developing flexible demonstrations that allow stakeholders to interact with the technology using their own data, fostering trust and answering critical questions about total cost of ownership, return on investment and alignment with objectives and key results. The chapter underscores how demos bridge the gap between theoretical potential and concrete understanding, build trust by showcasing reliable capabilities, spark imagination about future applications and even expose limitations. The chapter provides an extensive list of user interface prototyping platforms, AI-specific demonstration tools and user-computer interaction simulation software.*

There's no better way to communicate ideas than to create pilot demonstrations. You should demand that any AI idea headed toward an internal or external application be demoed. It's the best executive summary there is.

DOI:10.1201/9781003652748-12

Demonstration prototypes are essential to communicating innovation and "selling" the uniqueness of AI, ML and GenAI. You need to "see" what you're planning to design, develop and hopefully sell. You also need to see the technology in a problem-solving context.

One of the best ways to assess new business models, processes and technologies is to assess their potential in context, that is, how they could be deployed and how they could solve problems across multiple vertical industries and even disrupt business models and processes for competitive advantage. Scenarios, simulations and use cases can help assess and communicate potential. For example, your team might explain how an application might help an insurance company reach more customers, how a security tool works for a company's supply chain or how a social media listening technology can enhance data analytics.

These use cases must be specific and reflect precisely how the technology could be used to solve business problems or invent whole new business models and processes. "I'll show you what I mean," is a demo that describes what a product or service might do in the marketplace. Games and simulations can help assess impact before deployment. Supply chains can be animated, simulated and assessed. "What-if" questions can be asked and answered.

You should also develop live demonstrations that clearly indicate how your new company's products and services can be changed, improved or even disrupted. The demonstrations should be flexible. For example, if a prospective client or investor wants to see how machine learning works, he or she should be able to plug their data into a pipe that demonstrates how it works. Flexible demos are convincing. Canned demos sometimes beg too many questions, but should always be available when live demos fail.

# BOARD GRADE DEMOS

Demos should be "Board Grade," that is, understandable by Boards of Directors and other executives who comprehend business models/processes and AI technologies only at the highest level (which is a polite way of saying they usually barely comprehend technology). Said a little differently, business models/processes and technologies must be demystified (Andriole, 2023). Jargon and acronyms should be minimized. Examples should be straightforward and easy to understand. Demonstrating, for example, how a smart electronic payment system could accelerate collection, improve cash flow and generate interest income can be discussed and effectively communicated through an animated scenario. For many audiences, "demo" is the only language that makes sense. As suggested, demos should build upon scenario development, use case analyses and simulation to demonstrate the potential scalability of a new product or service to determine which AI investments make sense – and which don't.

Prospective clients can also better understand the potential of AI products and services with proactive assistance. Every client will ask a series of questions about any business model or technology you're considering. You should anticipate these questions and proactively answer clients' questions, including especially questions about total cost of ownership (TCO), return on investment (ROI) and objectives and key results (OKRs) – the triplets everyone loves. So demos are not just for you: they're also for your clients (and your investors).

Failing fast and failing cheap is a favorite executive investment strategy. Who doesn't love the idea of investing very little time and money to learn a lot in a very short period of time? Due diligence is a process that prospective clients should understand and implement whenever a demo graduates to pilot status. At that point, a series of questions should be asked as metrics are developed to empirically assess the contribution the model, process and technology might make to clients – which is precisely where demonstration prototypes can be leveraged!

Claude and I had a discussion about this: we both think demos play a critical role in technology adoption, especially for AI systems, for several compelling reasons:

> First, demos bridge the gap between abstract potential and concrete understanding. AI capabilities can be difficult to grasp conceptually, but a well-crafted demo transforms technical possibilities into tangible applications that people can immediately comprehend.
> The classic example is the iPhone introduction in 2007. Steve Jobs didn't just describe a touchscreen phone; he showed it working in real time, scrolling through music and making actual calls. That demonstration catalyzed a mobile revolution in a way specifications alone couldn't have.

For AI specifically, demos serve unique functions:

> They build trust by showing capabilities working reliably. When OpenAI demonstrated GPT models answering questions or GitHub Copilot writing code, it helped overcome skepticism about whether these systems could actually perform as claimed.
> A good demo doesn't just show what the technology does but opens mental models about what it could do in someone's specific context.

Demos also expose limitations realistically. Live demonstrations reveal where technologies struggle, which paradoxically can build credibility by setting appropriate expectations.

# DEMONSTRATION PLATFORMS AND TOOLS

The good news is that there are lots of tools you, your team – and your individual contributors – can use to demonstrate new ideas, products and services. We suggest you and your team look at the following:

**Figma/Figjam**: Create interactive UI prototypes with clickable elements that simulate real application flow. The prototype mode allows you to demonstrate user journeys without any coding.

**ProtoPie**: Build highly interactive prototypes that can respond to various inputs (touch, voice, sensor data) to demonstrate more complex AI-powered concepts.

**Framer**: Create interactive prototypes that look and feel like real applications. You can use their AI features to quickly generate UI components and layouts.

**Adobe XD**: Design and prototype user experiences with voice commands, animations and realistic interactions.

**Marvel App**: Simple but powerful prototyping tool that lets you create realistic app simulations.

**InVision**: Create interactive mockups that simulate real application functionality.

**Axure RP**: More advanced prototyping with conditional logic and dynamic content to simulate AI behaviors.

**Flinto**: Create prototypes with realistic transitions and interactions.

**Balsamiq**: For quick, low-fidelity wireframes to communicate basic concepts.

**Justinmind**: Create interactive wireframes and prototypes for web and mobile apps.

For AI-specific demonstrations, we like:

**Teachable Machine**: Create custom machine learning models in your browser to demonstrate AI capabilities without coding.

**RunwayML**: Use AI to generate and manipulate content in your demos.

**Voiceflow**: Design and prototype voice apps and conversational experiences.
**Durable AI**: Quickly create AI-powered websites and prototypes.

Microsoft also offers several tools within their ecosystem that are excellent for creating demonstration prototypes:

**Microsoft Power Apps**: A low-code platform that lets you build functional business applications quickly. You can integrate AI capabilities through AI Builder or Power Automate, making it ideal for demonstrating AI-enhanced business solutions.

**Microsoft Power BI**: For data visualization prototypes, Power BI can quickly create interactive dashboards that simulate AI-driven analytics.

**Microsoft Copilot Studio** (formerly Power Virtual Agents): Build and test conversational AI prototypes without requiring coding expertise.

**Microsoft Loop**: A collaborative canvas app that could be used to prototype collaborative AI experiences.

**Microsoft Designer**: AI-powered design tool that can help create visuals for your prototypes quickly.

**Microsoft Fabric**: An integrated analytics platform that includes AI capabilities for data-focused prototypes.

**Microsoft Mesh**: For mixed reality prototype experiences.

**Microsoft Fluid Framework**: Create collaborative experiences that could demonstrate AI-enhanced teamwork concepts.

**Microsoft Azure AI Studio**: If you need to demonstrate more sophisticated AI capabilities, this provides a visual interface for building and testing AI models.

**The Power Platform** (Power Apps, Power Automate, Power BI, Copilot Studio) would likely be your best bet within the Microsoft ecosystem for creating demonstration prototypes that look convincing while requiring minimal technical expertise. Would you like more specific information about any of these tools?

We think the easiest, fastest and least expensive tools include:

**Figma**: Free tier available, incredibly intuitive, huge template library and excellent for clickable prototypes. You can create convincing app mockups within hours, even as a beginner.

**Microsoft PowerPoint**: You likely already have access to it, has a minimal learning curve and can create surprisingly effective clickable prototypes through hyperlinks and animations.

**Teachable Machine**: Completely free, browser-based and lets you create working AI demos (image recognition, sound classification) in minutes without coding.

A balanced option?

**Microsoft Power Apps**: If you already have Microsoft 365, the learning curve is manageable, and you can create functional prototypes relatively quickly that look like real applications.

**Framer**: Their AI features can generate entire functional website prototypes from a text description in minutes.

If we had to pick just one that balances ease, speed and cost, we'd recommend Figma. Its free tier is generous, the learning curve is minimal and you can create highly convincing interactive prototypes that communicate your ideas effectively. You can have a basic prototype ready in a few hours.

When it comes to UCI (user-computer interaction) simulation tools, here are some ideas:

**Axure RP**: Offers advanced interaction design capabilities with conditional logic flows that can simulate complex UCI scenarios. Great for demonstrating sophisticated user interactions.

**Balsamiq**: Focuses on low-fidelity wireframing but includes interactive elements to simulate basic UCI flows. Perfect for quickly communicating fundamental interaction concepts.

**Adobe XD**: Provides excellent UCI prototyping capabilities with voice interactions, auto-animate features and user testing tools built in.

**UXPin**: Offers advanced interactive states and logic-based interactions that can demonstrate complex UCI flows.

**Principle**: Excellent for animating interface interactions and transitions.

**Proto.io**: Designed specifically for mobile app prototyping with realistic touch interactions.

**UserTesting**: While primarily a testing platform, it can be used to simulate how users would interact with your interface.

**InVision Studio**: Includes advanced animation and interaction design tools to simulate realistic user experiences.

If you're looking for tools that can simulate more complex user-computer interactions within the Microsoft ecosystem, Microsoft's Maquette (for mixed reality prototyping) or the human-computer interaction tools within Azure Cognitive Services might be good.

For creating demonstrations of AI product ideas specifically, these tools are pretty good.

For showcasing AI concepts without deep technical knowledge:

**Gradio**: Lets you build interactive demos for ML models in just a few lines of code. You can quickly wrap AI capabilities in a simple interface to demonstrate your concept.

**Streamlit**: Create interactive web applications around AI models with minimal coding. Particularly good for data-focused AI demonstrations.

**Teachable Machine by Google**: Create custom ML models (image recognition, audio classification) directly in your browser without writing code.

**RunwayML**: Provides access to powerful AI models through a visual interface. Great for demonstrating generative AI concepts.

**Hugging Face Spaces**: Deploy ML demos with a simple interface and share them publicly.

For simulating AI products before building them:

**Figma + AI Plugins** (like AI Mockup, Content Reel): Create interfaces that simulate AI functionality.

**Voiceflow**: Specifically for demonstrating conversational AI and voice assistant product ideas.

**Roboflow**: For computer vision product demos without deep technical knowledge.

**Elicit**: Research assistant that can help prototype AI research tools.

**Microsoft Copilot Studio**: Create chatbots and conversational interfaces without coding.

For more technical demonstrations your team might try:

**Jupyter Notebooks**: Create interactive, narrated demonstrations of AI functionality.

**Observable**: Create interactive, visual demonstrations of AI concepts.

**LangChain**: Framework for building applications with large language models.

We think that the combination of Streamlit (for functionality) and Figma (for UI) is particularly powerful for AI product demonstrations, allowing you to create convincing simulations of AI products without building the entire application. Streamlit is free, has an easy learning curve and can be deployed online to share with stakeholders.

This list is obviously too long. Your team can select a tool, build a prototype and then demo it to the powers that be – which includes you. Some of the tools are fast and easy, and some are very complicated.

The list is also intended to demonstrate something else, which is to show you just how many demo tools there are and how easy it is to find them with the help of the right partner. Here's something to think about: what if you hired a consultant to develop the list? What if you tasked your AI team to find all of the tools? Or what if you just asked Claude, Gemini or ChatGPT to develop the list – which is what I did? You can see how I prompted these partners with specific and different questions about exactly what I wanted, and how they responded with increasing specificity. Try it – and a few of the "easy" demo tools on the lists.

# Govern AI with Care

# 11

## ABSTRACT

*This chapter navigates the complex and often debated area of artificial intelligence (AI) governance. While acknowledging the intuitive urge and increasing pressure to establish formal frameworks for the organization and deployment of AI, it opens with a critical perspective on the potential pitfalls of overly rigid "governance," "standards" and "best practices." The chapter voices a common executive concern: that a zealous pursuit of externally imposed requirements, while necessary for compliance (e.g., digital security), can inadvertently stifle the very innovation that AI promises. The chapter then pivots to explore the components of AI governance as defined by current AI discourse, including ethical principles, regulatory compliance, bias management, transparency, accountability, data governance, risk management, human oversight and continuous monitoring. It further outlines the significant challenges associated with implementing effective AI governance, such as the lack of clear regulations, bias issues, transparency limitations and the need to balance innovation with control. The discussion then turns to the role of internal auditors in the AI governance landscape. While acknowledging their increasing interest and potential involvement in auditing AI frameworks, systems and use cases, the chapter maintains a pragmatic stance, questioning whether full-fledged, documented AI governance is always necessary.*

My feelings about artificial intelligence (AI) governance are mixed because "governance" like "standards," "maturity models" and "best practices" are potential straightjackets. Before you turn me in to the auditors, listen to my reasoning. Many

DOI:10.1201/9781003652748-13

companies work extensively to satisfy industry requirements set by someone else (like auditors and the "rules" they lobby). Some of the requirements are set by law, if not expectations about how your company performs a variety of tasks, like digital security. All good: you must adhere to these requirements. My concern is how distracting these requirements can be to your AI mission. So delegate all but the final signoff recognizing that AI governance is what it is.

Chat, Claude, Gemini and I discussed AI governance at some length. I asked them to analyze the whole AI governance process. Here's what we determined:

AI governance refers to the frameworks, policies and practices that guide the responsible development and use of AI. The principal components of AI governance include:

1. Ethical Principles and Guidelines
2. Regulatory Compliance and Legal Frameworks
3. Bias and Fairness Management
4. Transparency and Explainability
5. Accountability and Oversight
6. Data Governance and Privacy Protection
7. Risk Management and Security
8. Human-in-the-Loop and AI Oversight
9. Continuous Monitoring and Impact Assessment

Challenges?

1. Lack of Clear Regulations and Standards
2. Bias and Fairness Issues
3. Transparency and Explainability
4. Data Privacy and Security Concerns
5. Defining Accountability and Responsibility
6. Integration with Existing Corporate Policies
7. Balancing Innovation with Regulation
8. Skill Gaps and Expertise Shortages
9. Risk of AI Misuse and Unintended Consequences
10. Continuous Monitoring and Evolving AI Risks

You need to understand both the key components of AI governance and the major challenges associated with implementing it effectively. A well-structured AI governance framework is essential to mitigate risks, ensure ethical compliance and maintain a competitive edge. Here's what we think you should focus on:

- **Ethical Principles and Guidelines**: AI must align with fairness, accountability, transparency and human-centric values to prevent unethical outcomes.

- **Regulatory Compliance and Legal Frameworks**: Companies must navigate global AI regulations (e.g., GDPR, EU AI Act, U.S. AI policy) and ensure compliance.
- **Bias and Fairness Management**: Identifying and mitigating biases in AI models is crucial to ensuring fair treatment across diverse populations.
- **Transparency and Explainability**: AI decisions must be interpretable to stakeholders, regulators and customers to build trust.
- **Accountability and Oversight**: Clear responsibility must be assigned for AI decision-making, with governance boards or ethics committees overseeing compliance.
- **Data Governance and Privacy Protection**: AI systems must adhere to strict data protection laws while ensuring secure data usage.
- **Risk Management and Security**: AI models must be monitored for potential misuse, cybersecurity risks and unintended consequences.
- **Human-in-the-Loop and Oversight**: High-risk AI applications should include human decision-makers to prevent overreliance on automation.
- **Continuous Monitoring and Impact Assessment**: AI models require ongoing evaluation to detect bias, maintain ethical integrity and adapt to new regulations.

So what should you do?

- **Invest in AI Governance Teams**: Establish dedicated teams or ethics committees to oversee AI compliance.
- **Develop Clear AI Policies**: Define internal AI guidelines and ensure alignment with regulatory expectations.
- **Prioritize Ethical AI**: Embed fairness, transparency and accountability into AI development and decision-making.
- **Balance Innovation and Compliance**: Encourage AI-driven growth while implementing safeguards against ethical and legal risks.
- **Foster Cross-Department Collaboration**: AI governance should involve legal, compliance, IT, HR and executive leadership to ensure a holistic approach.
- **Stay Ahead of Regulations**: Monitor global AI laws and proactively adjust governance frameworks to meet new requirements.

Process discipline is easier said than done. Nothing new here. You may talk a good project management game, for example, but I wonder how many of your projects the Project Management Institute (PMI) would say are done correctly. It's the same for software development, sales processes and consulting best practices. They all look good during training, but not so much in the field.

AI governance has lots of moving parts. There are consultants everywhere screaming about how badly you need "governance" around your AI initiatives. Of course they are: AI governance is another revenue stream. But at the end of the day – and you know this as an executive – governance is more of a concept than a best practice that saves or makes you money – unless it's "required" by the auditors and their minions. In that case, it's an expense.

# GOVERNANCE WITH AUDITORS

What about those auditors? Do they require an AI governance policy? What's internal audit's role in AI governance? What do they want? EY sees it this way (Rodgers and Thomas, 2025):

*Gaining a seat at the table around AI governance.*

*Auditing the performance of the AI framework and governance, as well as AI systems and products.*

*Raising the enterprise IQ around responsible AI.*

These are the kinds of suggestions auditors like to make – to make themselves relevant and eventually perhaps control the initiatives they believe fall within their purview of responsibilities. Here's the current thinking (Rodgers and Thomas, 2025):

*Internal audit faces challenges in managing AI risks, requiring a proactive approach to governance.*

*Chief audit executives should develop annual AI audit plans, educate teams on risks and integrate AI governance into frameworks to promote responsible use.*

*Collaboration with executive leaders and risk committees is essential for effective AI oversight.*

Here's where it's all going (Paloalto, 2025):

*Regulatory frameworks play a central role in AI governance by ensuring compliance with relevant laws and industry standards. As AI technologies continue to advance, governments and regulatory bodies develop new regulations to address emerging challenges. Enterprises must stay abreast of these evolving requirements and incorporate them into their governance structures.*

Gemini insisted on summarizing things:

> *While a broad legal mandate for AI audits doesn't yet exist in the United States, the trend is towards greater regulatory scrutiny. Emerging laws, particularly in the EU and at the state level, are introducing requirements that necessitate audit-like processes, especially for high-risk AI applications. Proactive organizations will adopt robust AI governance frameworks that include regular evaluation and monitoring to ensure compliance, mitigate risks, and build trust in their AI systems.*

Are you proactive?

# GOVERNANCE IN THE TRENCHES

All good, but you may not even need an AI governance structure with an explicit, documented governance policy that you must enforce. Belli (2025) offers some perspective:

> *While audits are becoming a core feature of working with AI, they don't have a predetermined process ... specifically, audits often face four core challenges: 1) they don't follow a straight line, 2) data governance is messy, 3) they require internal trust, and 4) they focus on the past.*

Maybe, just maybe you don't need an AI governance policy at all (Hutchins and Botkin, 2024):

> *If a company's use of AI is minimal and doesn't involve substantial data processing or decision-making, a detailed governance policy may be unnecessary. In such cases, adherence to existing data protection and ethical guidelines may suffice.*

They go further with a checklist of conditions when an AI governance policy may be unnecessary:
- *Low-risk environments*
- *Temporary or experimental AI projects*
- *Outsourced AI services*
- *Small-business operations*

The decision about whether or not to invest in the development and enforcement of an AI governance policy is straightforward. If you're still in the early stages of AI application development with limited deployments, a formal AI governance policy is probably unnecessary. But watch the regulations here. It may get harder to define and implement your AI agenda as it grows.

# Watch the Regulators

# 12

## ABSTRACT

*This chapter looks at AI regulation, exploring the inherent tension between the profit-driven embrace of AI technologies like machine learning and generative AI, and the societal anxieties surrounding truth, reality and potential harms. Recognizing a growing consensus for the necessity of some form of AI management, it navigates the complex reality of current regulatory efforts, noting the pioneering actions in regions like the EU and China, while acknowledging the unique challenges facing the U.S., including legislative hurdles and industry (lobbying) influence. The chapter points to nascent legislative initiatives at the federal level in the U.S., suggesting a potential for future regulation, possibly driven by state-level action or international collaborations. It unpacks particularly thorny issues that complicate regulation, such as copyright and intellectual property rights related to AI-generated content, as well as the legal ambiguities surrounding the "fair use" of training data.*

Those who use AI, machine learning and GenAI to make money – no matter how it's made – love AI. Those who worry about truth and reality may hate what AI can do. (No one can plead ignorance.) Facebook's algorithms that threaten the mental well-being of young women is a perfect example of how machine learning algorithms can increase advertising dollars while harming its clients. AI will improve these algorithms. On the other hand, AI might help cure cancer.

There are lots of us who believe that some form of regulation is necessary. Some countries are already well on their way to legislative control

(Dans, 2023). At the very least, AI technology – like all technology – must be "managed."

ChatGPT knows exactly what to do. I reviewed these suggestions and found them to be right on the money. See what you think:

**Establish Clear Ethical Guidelines**: Governments, industries and institutions should collaborate to establish ethical guidelines to ensure the responsible development and use of generative AI. These guidelines should address issues such as privacy, security, transparency and accountability.

**Require Transparency**: Generative AI systems should be designed to be transparent, meaning that their decision-making processes should be clear and understandable. Developers should be required to provide explanations of how their systems work and how they make decisions.

**Implement Data Privacy Laws**: Generative AI systems rely on vast amounts of data to learn and improve. Regulations should be in place to protect individuals' privacy rights and ensure that data is collected and used ethically and legally.

**Create Oversight Agencies**: There should be agencies responsible for overseeing the development and deployment of generative AI systems. These agencies should have the authority to review and approve or reject new systems, and to investigate any issues or complaints that arise.

**Encourage Collaboration**: The development and use of generative AI should be a collaborative effort between government, industry, academia and the public. These stakeholders should work together to identify and address potential ethical, social and legal issues.

**Ensure Accountability**: Generative AI developers and users should be held accountable for any negative consequences that result from their systems. There should be a system in place to monitor and regulate the use of these systems, with appropriate penalties for noncompliance.

Gemini agrees with the following:

**Content Moderation**: Governments could require companies that use generative AI to moderate the content that is generated. This could involve filtering out harmful or offensive content, or requiring users to verify their identity before generating content.

**Transparency**: Governments could require companies that use generative AI to be transparent about how their systems work. This would allow users to understand how their data is being used and to make informed decisions about whether or not to interact with generative AI systems.

**Education**: Governments could educate the public about the potential risks and benefits of generative AI. This would help people to understand how to use generative AI responsibly and to be aware of the potential harms that it could cause.

**Research**: Governments could fund research into the development of generative AI that is safe and ethical. This would help to ensure that generative AI is used in a way that benefits society and does not harm individuals or groups.

There's a political aspect of regulation that we all must acknowledge. The Biden administration had a very different perspective about regulation than the Trump administration. So your perspective may be very different from what the bots recommended above. Your call. But I agree with the bots: we need some regulation.

Those who want to "pause" have their list too (Future of Life Institute, 2023):

- *Mandate robust third-party auditing and certification*
- *Regulate access to computational power*
- *Establish capable AI agencies at the national level*
- *Establish liability for AI-caused harms*
- *Introduce measures to prevent and track AI model leaks*
- *Expand technical AI safety research funding*
- *Develop standards for identifying and managing AI-generated content and recommendations*

# PROGRESS OR PARALYSIS

The U.S. faces a number of somewhat unique regulatory challenges ranging from the technology ignorance of lawmakers to lobbyists who own much of the legislative process. In addition to these challenges are partisan politics and dubious relationships that many U.S. lawmakers have with the companies and industries they're expected to regulate. While it's impossible to predict if the U.S. will meaningfully regulate AI, machine learning and generative AI, there are signs – even with the challenges – that progress is at least possible, though temporarily stalled for at least another few years.

Some U.S. states – such as California and New York – may take the lead. It may be that a bottom-up regulatory approach will be more effective than a federal top-down approach, but that remains to be seen. State-by-state regulations will complicate cross-border commerce which is why a federal approach may be necessary. Partnerships with contiguous countries might also offer some regulatory promise. Canada, for example, introduced the *Artificial Intelligence and Data Act* (AIDA) in 2022 which could form the basis of a NAFTA-like agreement among Canada, Mexico and the U.S., though, here too, there are some new challenges that may stall all this for a few years (which could change over time, even abruptly).

Beyond the politics around federal regulation, there are some unusually challenging issues that may paralyze regulatory efforts simply because of their complexity. Should artists be compensated if GenAI mimics their work? New challenges around copyright and intellectual property rights are far from understood and definitely unresolved.

There are additional challenges that must be managed. Fried (2023) begins her analysis with a blunt headline: "generative AI is a legal minefield." She identifies at least one major legal challenge:

> *Getty, for example, is suing Stable Diffusion, saying the open-source AI image generator trained its engine on 12 million images from Getty's database without getting permission or providing compensation.*

The National Institute of Standards (NIST) entered the regulatory picture (NIST, 2023) providing, as NIST always does, a set of suggestions about how to proceed with standards:

> *NIST launched the Trustworthy and Responsible AI Resource Center, which will facilitate implementation of, and international alignment with, the AI RMF ... NIST (also) released the AI Risk Management Framework.*

Technology is clearly moving faster than the regulators can walk or talk – and faster than they *want* to walk or talk. While there are efforts underway to regulate AI, machine learning and GenAI, there are also efforts to delay or avoid any kind of regulation. It's safe to say that the world is both confused and challenged by this technology. Many regulatory drafts have been developed and shared, but anything final or permanent has yet to be created. One especially challenging aspect of regulation is enforcement. What happens when some individual, some company or some country violates regulations? While the European Union (EU) actively fines companies that violate its privacy and data sharing laws, the U.S. is a regulatory weakling.

## WATCH CLOSELY

Regulatory climates and policies can change quickly. So much regulatory action depends upon how quickly the power of AI is revealed, feared and praised. We know, for example, that orders of performance magnitude separate the chatbots. What capabilities will ChatGPT 10 have? As more and more industries, functions and processes yield to large language models and agentic AI, there will be additional pressure to "regulate" at some level. On the other hand, if there's sufficient coverage of the limitations of AI and a few high-profile regulations that quell the major fears, then broad regulatory efforts will likely collapse. No one knows for sure. Sadly, way too much regulatory analysis is now political, not an issue about what's right or good.

As suggested, decisions around regulation will not be completely anchored in technology capabilities. Social, political and economic concerns about the impact of regulation will exert as much if not more influence upon whatever regulatory scenarios emerge. This changes the game, the players and the rules. All of the activity around draft and proposed regulations have several filters through which they must pass. This means that meaningful legislation will be slow to proceed. It's also likely that the U.S. will lose the regulatory game to other countries that are already outpacing U.S.'s regulatory efforts. If your company is global, you need to pay attention to the regulatory arms races and how the countries you deal with are regulating AI. Fines can hurt: in 2023 Meta paid the EU $1.3B in fines.

While regulatory predictions are impossible to make, it's safe to say that there will be a lag between regulatory policy and the growing power of AI. This means that regulations will lag applications for years and perhaps even permanently. This happens when technology moves as fast as AI is moving – and is likely to move in the future. The old ways of treading lightly in the regulatory world will not work for AI. Treating this technology as just another incremental advance is a mistake that the U.S. regulatory apparatus will probably make. That warning aside, all of this assumes that there's a real desire to regulate the technology. While there may be an honest desire to regulate the technology in several countries and a few U.S. states, it remains to be seen if the U.S. is capable of developing and enforcing impactful federal regulations of a fast-moving technology target. (It's noteworthy that the U.S. has not attempted to regulate social media.) You need to track this closely because regulation will affect the way you use AI.

## LIKELY OR NOT, HERE IT COMES

I asked Grok to summarize it all:

**Federal Policy**: Expect continued emphasis on voluntary guidelines, infrastructure investment and national security-focused AI development, with minimal new regulations. Existing laws (e.g., FTC's authority over deceptive practices) will be stretched to cover AI issues.

**State Dominance**: States will drive AI regulation, particularly on consumer protection, transparency and sector-specific applications. This will create compliance challenges but address local concerns like discrimination or environmental impact.

**Private Sector Role**: Companies may adopt self-regulatory measures to preempt state laws or align with global standards, especially for generative AI. Industry-led frameworks could fill gaps left by federal inaction.

**Legal Battles**: without clear federal guidance, courts will increasingly resolve AI-related disputes (e.g., copyright, bias), potentially setting de facto standards.

So what should you do?

Monitor state legislation closely, especially in high-activity states like California, Colorado and New York.

Implement NIST's AI Risk Management Framework voluntarily to prepare for potential future standards.

Conduct regular risk assessments for AI systems, particularly those affecting hiring, finance or healthcare, to align with state consumer protection laws.

Engage with industry groups to shape self-regulatory frameworks that could influence policy.

Watch the Trump administration's deregulatory push against the backdrop of state-level activism and global pressures. The lack of a unified federal policy could lead to inefficiencies or missed opportunities to address AI's risks.

It remains to be seen what U.S. regulators do, if they do anything. But regardless of how you see all this playing out, you have no choice but to track it carefully.

There's another aspect of all this you should consider. As your approach to AI evolves, you might consider where you want to land regarding regulatory priorities. Where do you stand? Do you want more federal AI regulation or are you more comfortable with the states taking the lead? Are you a nuanced executive who never takes strong positions? Or do you have a point of view you want to share? Is this even relevant to how you should think about AI?

You need to decide where you want to be on the regulatory continuum. You need to decide what the best place is for your business and what the best place is for your conscience.

# PART III

# Executive Awareness

# Good and Bad AI

# 13

## ABSTRACT

*This chapter examines the dual nature of artificial intelligence (AI) as it matures from experimental technology to a strategic enterprise asset. The "good" trajectory shows AI evolving beyond hype into substantive business transformation: machine learning applications will proliferate across routine business processes. Executives will develop deeper conceptual understanding of AI capabilities, generative AI tools will revolutionize knowledge work, ROI metrics will evolve into strategic OKRs, and educational institutions will fundamentally redesign curricula to address AI's disruptive impact. The chapter also explores AI's "dark side" in the absence of meaningful regulation: the unprecedented scaling of misinformation campaigns through increasingly sophisticated AI-generated content, the blurring ethical boundaries between productivity tools and academic/professional "cheating" and the alarming expansion of AI-powered cyberattacks targeting enterprise systems.*

AI, machine learning (ML) and especially generative AI (GenAI) are everywhere. But lots of the attention is performance art, not substance: when the media falls in love with a technology story it becomes "breaking news" and "news alerts" every day, all day long. AI is like commercials for Medicare advantage policies: endlessly repetitive, ICYMI and FOMO – only to be replaced by ubiquitous messages ordering us to buy lots of AI.

DOI:10.1201/9781003652748-16

# GOOD AI

Here are five "good" predictions we can make about AI:

1. Machine learning will explode
2. Executives will focus on AI
3. ChatGPT, Claude and all the rest will invade everything
4. ROI will become strategic objectives and key results (OKRs)
5. Universities will rethink curriculum

## Machine Learning Will Explode

Simple applications of ML (narrow AI/supervised learning) will continue to explode on the problem-solving scene. While everyone expects GenAI to continue to dominate the conversation – *which it will* – there will also be an unprecedented number of "simple" applications of ML. Why? Part of the reason is because executives like you have learned to pay attention to AI, ML and GenAI. Narrow AI/supervised learning applications are well-bounded and regression-solvable problems are also cheap to develop and easy to deploy. In order to find these opportunities, companies will finally spend some money on business process modeling and process mining to identify the most promising applications. Everything routine and repeatable is the target. All of the awareness around AI will pay huge dividends for the automation, replacement and reimagination of business processes across your company. You need to revisit that process inventory and start matching problem processes with simple ML algorithms. Call those individual contributors back into your real or virtual office and set them free.

## Executives Will Understand AI

While many executives – including maybe you – may not understand technology the way they should (Andriole, 2023), their interest in all things "AI" will continue to grow. Because of all the hype and all of the FOMO warnings, executives will educate themselves about how AI works – at a conceptual, not computer science-based level – and the problems AI can solve. You will do this because you will be seduced by the possibilities of making money *and* saving money with AI. You will also do this because you will – for the first time – begin to integrate AI, ML and GenAI into you strategic thinking. If AI is truly strategic, you have no choice but to understand how it works and what it does – which is perhaps why you bought this book!

# ChatGPT, Claude, Gemini and All the Rest Will Invade Everything

You have not scratched the surface of the problems GenAI will solve – not by the end of the decade, but within the next two or three years. Way too many companies will wake from the technology dead to discover a really powerful technology that can save them time and money – *lots of time and money* – and make their companies more competitive. They will also discover that ChatGPT, Claude, Gemini, Dall-E, Synthesia, Midjourney, Suno, Sora and all the rest can make them richer.

As I have said over and over again, the range of applications is literally endless. Where will impact be felt? All of the so-called knowledge industries will – for the first time in their lives – find themselves in the crosshairs of AI, ML and GenAI, including paralegals, accountants, marketers, traders, bankers, customer service representatives and media professionals, among so many others identified in this book. Listen to what McKinsey (Ellingrud et al., 2023) has to say about it:

> *By 2030, activities that account for up to 30 percent of hours currently worked across the US economy could be automated – a trend accelerated by generative AI.*

TechTarget (Lutkevich, 2024) describes it this way:

> *In past automation-fueled labor fears, machines would automate tedious, repetitive work. Generative AI is different in that it automates creative tasks such as writing, coding and even music making.*

# ROI Will Become OKRs

AI, ML and GenAI will evolve from "science projects" to MVPs (minimal viable products) that will suggest initial ROIs that will translate into OKRs. The transition from simple ROI calculations to OKRs will solidify AI's integration into enterprise strategy. When AI/ML/GenAI becomes seriously "strategic," its role will fundamentally change. Every single perspective that "AI" has been overhyped, that it will only have limited impact, and that certain professions will be immune to its effects will be exposed as fake news.

# Universities Will Rethink Curriculum

For decades – even centuries – universities created academic disciplines, "majors" and "minors" designed to prepare their students for successful careers.

They believed their curriculum would persist over time, which explains why some university curriculum has remained essentially static for decades. The closest thing to a radical challenge to the structure and content of curriculum occurred when the Internet arrived. When it hit in full force, there was some serious thinking about how "e" everything would land – which it obviously did – but many universities treated the Internet as just another competitive tool until they fully understand its role as a transaction platform – about ten years after the dot.com crash. GenAI is different. It's a replacement, and it's moving fast.

Many academic disciplines and the courses that define them are already obsolete. The typical courses in these disciplines limped into ML over the past ten years but have largely ignored the real impact that AI, ML and GenAI will inevitably have on all things business. Universities will begin to look seriously at the impact, AI, ML and GenAI will have on its curriculum and begin to rethink its entire curriculum. They have no choice – which is a very good thing.

This also enables you to recruit graduates with the right skills just the way the so-called Big Four accounting firms – EY, Deloitte, PWC and KPMG – recruit business students who understand accounting and ideally have earned their CPA certifications. Instead of expertise in dying fields (!), colleges and universities need to prepare students for careers in AI, ML and GenAI so you can hire the talent you need.

## AI Will Mature

The five predictions described here are among others that describe how AI, ML and GenAI will leave adolescence. The most important one discussed here is AI's new strategic assignment. Once a technology begins to play this role, its status changes. It receives funding, talent is recruited and products and services are defined through its capabilities. AI, ML and GenAI will play a whole new strategic role in the enterprise, which guarantees its permanent status, as if there was ever any doubt.

But there's another aspect of maturity that needs to be discussed. "AI" will undoubtedly morph a hundred ways over the next few years. It will not only become more powerful, but its role will become more prominent in C-Suites, with Boards, investors and the analysts who cover public companies. This prominence will forever change the way AI is discussed and evaluated as a strategic driver.

# BAD AI

Bad AI can be really bad. Without impactful regulation – which will not happen any time soon in the U.S. – bad AI will get much worse. So here's a short list of how bad AI can – and will – get without regulation. Those who believe AI will be incrementally bad are naive. Let's look at just three ways AI is already bad.

# Misinformation and Disinformation Will Continue to Explode

AI is the best misinformation and disinformation machine the world has ever seen – and it's getting smarter, faster and cheaper. The automation of increasingly complex and effective misinformation and disinformation is proceeding on schedule for those who want to weaponize the technology. "Fake news" is just the tip of the iceberg. Much more sophisticated activities are well underway – have been for years – that undermine "truth" and "objectivity" in every possible way. Propaganda is now digital. Can you imagine how weird – and effective – this can get? Listen to this example described by Pranshu Verma (2023):

> One AI-generated article recounted a made-up story about Benjamin Netanyahu's psychiatrist, a NewsGuard investigation found, alleging that he had died and left behind a note suggesting the involvement of the Israeli prime minister … the claim was … spread by users on TikTok, Reddit and Instagram.

How bad can it get (Verma, 2023)?

> Well-dressed AI-generated news anchors are spewing pro-Chinese propaganda, amplified by bot networks sympathetic to Beijing. In Slovakia, politicians up for election found their voices had been cloned to say controversial things they never uttered, days before voters went to the polls.

Without significant legislation, this kind of activity will grow.

# Cheaters Rejoice (But What's "Cheating"?)

Cheaters love ChatGPT, Gemini, Claude and all the rest. It makes their lives easier. If you haven't already tried to "cheat" with large language models you're behind the curve. Students started "cheating" in 2022 and ChatGPT has made their lives easier ever since, but here's a twist (Nam, 2023):

*In addition to being most likely to use AI tools, business majors are least likely to say that using AI tools to complete assignments or exams is cheating or plagiarism.*

This means that using tools like ChatGPT is becoming acceptable.

Marketing professionals can develop press releases and marketing campaigns. Professors can use ChatGPT to write syllabi and case studies. Project managers can ask for help.

But the real question is about "cheating" itself. What is it?

An important way to think about the role that GenAI can play is to develop a "task participation continuum." "Automation" is now commonplace. Full partnerships have arrived. Why in the world would you forbid your marketing team to work with these tools? It makes absolutely no sense. On the other hand, what if marketing teams only used these tools to do their work?

The relationship between task complexity and its "assignment" is still developing. The questions "how complex is the task?" and "who does the work?" are good questions today, but over time the relationship will change. What's considered "human" – *and ethical* – today will change as GenAI develops. Task complexity will also be redefined as the number of use GenAI cases increases. Watch this one carefully: "cheating" will likely be redefined as "consulting" or "partnering" in just a few years. *The distinction between cheating and productivity will blur and eventually disappear altogether – if it hasn't already.*

# CYBERATTACKS WILL MULTIPLY

Databases, processes, content – you name it – are the targets of cyberattacks. AI will expand the number of targets and the effectiveness of the attacks. Morgan Stanley (2024) lists some threats:

*Cybercriminals exploit AI to improve the algorithms they use for deciphering passwords.*

*Doctored content can ... be broadly distributed online in seconds – including on influential social media platforms.*

*Hackers 'poison' or alter the training data used by an AI algorithm to influence the decisions it ultimately makes.*

While AI enables cyberattacks, it can also be used to thwart attacks.

# BAD TO WORSE, UNLESS

AI, ML and GenAI can hurt you. But they can also help you. While balance makes intuitive sense, it should not be the desired outcome. The good must outweigh the bad. How we get there is another question altogether. Part of the answer is regulation even though most analysts do not believe the U.S. will develop and enforce meaningful regulation. In fact, and as we've already noted, legislation may well come from U.S. states before the U.S. implements federal legislation.

# Donald Trump and Taylor Swift **14**

---

## ABSTRACT

*This chapter examines the growing threat of AI-generated misinformation and disinformation, using high-profile political incidents as case studies to illustrate potential executive vulnerabilities. Through detailed analysis of Donald Trump's use of falsified Taylor Swift endorsements and other AI-generated content during the 2024 presidential campaign, the chapter demonstrates how easily AI can be weaponized to create persuasive false narratives. The chapter frames AI-generated disinformation not merely as a political or celebrity problem, but as an emerging business threat that executives must address. It concludes with the importance of "malice management."*

Here's a case of bad AI. It's about one of the most recognizable celebrities on the planet: Taylor Swift. Who wouldn't want her endorsement for anything? Given the value of that endorsement, how might a politician get it? Well, the politician could just ask her. Or persuade some friends who know her to ask for the endorsement. Another way to get the endorsement is to just act like you already have it *by faking it*. It's a good lesson for all of us and one that you should learn because you too can become victim to similar activities.
Rachel Looker (2024) from the BBC explained what happened:

> *Donald Trump appears to have falsely implied he has Taylor Swift's endorsement, posting fake images on social media.*
> *The Republican presidential candidate posted the message "I accept!" alongside the images, which were taken from other social media accounts. Many appear to have been created using artificial intelligence.*

DOI:10.1201/9781003652748-17

According to Dan Merica and Ali Swenson from the Associated Press published on ABC News Online (2024):

> *Former President Donald Trump has been active on his social accounts ... but many of his posts don't have much to do with reality.*
>
> *He posted a fake image of someone who looks like Vice President Kamala Harris addressing what appears to be a communist rally in Chicago.*

Marianna Spring (2024) of the BBC noted in March how Trump also uses fake images to persuade Black voters to support his candidacy. There are "dozens of fakes portraying black Trump supporters." One of the images (of Trump and some young Black men) "was widely viewed on social media with a caption saying Trump had stopped his motorcade to pose with these men."

# AI ENABLERS

Unfortunately, this kind of disinformation is way too easy to create and disseminate. Once a fake image, video or audio is created, and especially if it's salacious enough, it goes viral. This one/two punch is now standard procedure for some marketing teams around political candidates (and movie stars, musicians, athletes, executives, etc.). Research indicates that fake images and videos are dangerous (deVos, 2024).

So how easy is it to fake?

Suffice it to say that an eighth grader could easily produce amazing fake images, as well as animated deep or "light" fakes in a minutes. The Center for Countering Digital Hate (Wendling, 2024) tested four of the largest public-facing AI platforms: Midjourney, OpenAI's ChatGPT Plus, Stability.ai's DreamStudio and Microsoft's Image Creator for their ability to create fake images. About 60% of the tests were successful. There are also tools for creating deep fakes with animation and audio as well.

# AI WAY OF LIFE – FOR SOME

Politicians – as well as anyone with a high profile who wants to create some effect or achieve some specific outcome – can use fake images, videos and audios to achieve their objectives. The tools are getting cheaper, faster and better, and the number of skilled fakers is exploding.

Trump is not the only politician to use fake images, videos and audios. Mark Scott (2024) reported in Politico that there are lots of offenders:

*"In Moldova, President Maia Sandu has been repeatedly targeted with AI-generated deepfakes to ridicule both her personally and her pro-Western government."*

*"Russian-linked groups also created ... an AI-generated Tom Cruise criticizing the upcoming Paris Olympics via a spoofed Netflix documentary."*

---

# NOW WHAT?

---

Because there are over 4,000 celebrities who have been victims of deepfake pornography and other deepfake damage (Badshah, 2024), there's a celebrity populist movement to combat the use of fake images and deepfakes. Their weapons are awareness, publicity and lawsuits. Legislation – the "DEEPFAKES Accountability Act" – has been proposed to regulate the use of deepfakes, but according to Graham (2024) "currently, there is no comprehensive enacted federal legislation in the United States that bans or even regulates deepfakes." Labeling AI-generated content is on old idea that without enforcement teeth is just getting older. There are also tools we can use to detect deepfakes (Dunham, 2023). But the tools are still not effective enough to detect all fake images, videos and audios, and there's no mandatory use of any detection tools.

Here's the situation. We have a set of tools capable of generating fake images, fake videos and fake audios, and these tools have never been easier, cheaper or faster to use. The tools are irresistible to those who want to distort reality for their own purposes. The U.S. government – unlike some European governments – has failed to enact legislation that regulates deepfakes (or much of anything around AI). So the battle is a DIY one. Those attacked and damaged must fight on their own behalf with whatever tools they can find. Until the do-it-yourselfers get some regulatory help, "fake" will remain a viable tool for those willing to distort reality for their own purposes. So pay close attention to what you see and hear because it might just be fake.

Why is all this important to you? It's important because misinformation, disinformation, deepfakes and other AI malice may come home to haunt you – if they haven't already. Cynically, you can also abuse it for your own nefarious purposes. You cannot avoid it and you cannot "rise above it" because it will find you, your products and your services. Your competitors may use misinformation, disinformation, deepfakes and other AI malice against you. Sadly, the management of malice is now a core competency. Executives in their own worlds are also "celebrities" who must know how to create and control misinformation, disinformation and deepfakes.

There's a thin line, by the way, between what companies say about their products and services, and fake news. Marketing professionals routinely "exaggerate" the capabilities of their products and services. This is what marketing teams are paid to do. So there's more than a hint of hypocrisy about what advertising and marketing does all day and complaints about misinformation, disinformation and that lovely term that floods the airways every day: fake news. Your products and services are also regularly attacked by your competitors who in one way or another accuse you of lying about what your company does as well as about you and the management team that runs it. Competition is a blood sport, and everyone says lots of things that aren't completely true about their competitors and their leaders. AI can "help" here too. So you have some decisions to make.

# Track Major Technology Trends

# 15

## ABSTRACT

*This chapter examines the critical role that technology tracking plays in corporate success. The chapter addresses the troubling digital literacy gap among executive leadership, citing research showing only 7% of large companies have digitally savvy executive teams – with particularly concerning deficiencies among CEOs (23%) and CFOs (12%). The chapter concludes by advocating for a proactive approach to technology understanding, where executives develop the core competency of "matching" specific technologies to business problems rather than delegating this critical function. It describes technology literacy as a fundamental requirement for effective leadership in the digital age.*

Every year the Gartner Group – perhaps the premier technology research organization – releases its list of technology trends. The 2025 (Alvarez, 2024) list looked like this (organized in three buckets). Look at what's #1:

Bucket #1: AI Imperatives and Risks

- Agentic AI
- AI Governance Platforms
- Disinformation Security

Bucket #2: New Frontiers of Computing

- Post-quantum Cryptography
- Ambient Invisible Intelligence

DOI:10.1201/9781003652748-18

- Energy-Efficient Computing
- Hybrid Computing

Bucket #3: Human Machine Synergy

- Spatial Computing
- Polyfunctional Robots
- Neurological Enhancement

# BUCKETS

What's good about this list are the buckets. It's impossible *not* to group them together to explain larger trajectories of the technologies likely to impact all aspects of business. So organizing the trends as buckets makes sense.

The AI bucket is right – and my students would agree. In our classes on AI, machine learning (ML) and generative AI (GenAI), and emerging business technologies, at the Villanova School of Business, we also track technology trends. We move from LLMs to GPTs to custom GPTs to light language models to agentic AI pretty quickly noting how "easy" it is to create agents with tools like Autogen, LangChain, Zapier and CrewAI, among others. There's no question that agentic AI is a major and significant trend. As we've discussed throughout this book, understanding AI, ML and GenAI is essential if you want your company to remain competitive.

AI governance (see Chapter 10) is necessary, but not always so easily defined or enforced. Gartner is correct to list this technology trend. But as they note, "AI guidelines vary across regions and industries, making it difficult to establish consistent practices."

One of the major challenges of AI is its ability to create and disseminate disinformation. As Gartner suggests, "disinformation security" is not only an important trend, it's a necessity.

The second bucket – new frontiers of computing – maps nearly perfecting onto our emerging business technologies course. Post-quantum cryptography – "data protection that is resistant to quantum computing (QC) decryption risks" – anticipates progress in quantum computing which is inevitable and at times risky. It will also accelerate the power of AI exponentially. So track it.

Our reaction to ambient invisible intelligence trends is "it's about time" we started talking about using technology to create natural, intuitive experiences.

Energy-efficient computing is a requirement that's exploding. While blockchain was the wake-up call about energy requirements, AI is the tsunami. Gartner is right to highlight this requirement regardless of how it's satisfied.

The hybrid computing trend is obvious.

The third bucket – human machine synergy – is another one that's overdue. The first trend here is spatial computing, which resurrects augmented and virtual reality to solve some of the problems we expected it to solve five years ago. The enabling technology is now ready to exploit this technology in areas that Gartner identifies, like "gaming, education and e-commerce … healthcare, retail and manufacturing."

While Gartner identifies the cost and unwieldy nature of head-mounted displays, we believe these displays will shrink considerably in the next few years.

Gartner identifies "polyfunctional robots" as an important trend and we agree. The marriage between robotics and AI has just begun and will soon yield children capable of performing multiple tasks. If you're in that industry, exploit this marriage.

Many years ago (From the Interface, 2020) the Defense Advanced Research Projects Agency (DARPA) invested in brain computer interfaces. In fact, decades ago, DARPA funded some of the earliest research in biocybernetics (The Back Vault, 1997). Companies like Neuralink have already demonstrated significant potential here. Gartner correctly puts neurological enhancement on the list of technology trends to watch. AI algorithms power all these trends.

Gartner's buckets map closely with the trends we track at the university. Our *AI, ML and Gen AI* and *emerging business technologies* courses overlap with many of Gartner's trends. You should follow Gartner's lead and organize them into baskets.

# THE TECHNOLOGY TRENDS BUSINESS

Gartner is not the only company that focuses on technology trends. Forrester, Deloitte, IBM, IDC, PWC and others track and predict technology trends. The challenge of course is the volatility of these trends. The courses we teach at the university are, for example, redesigned every semester. In 2020, GenAI was unrecognizable as an application platform. Today it's displacing industries. Where will it be in five years? The same is true about agentic AI.

Trends forecasters should also identify where the technologies will land across the vertical industries and the processes and subprocesses that define them. They should also probabilistically identify the processes and subprocesses that will be automated, improved or eliminated as AI, ML and GenAI evolves.

This would enable strategists, tacticians – and you – to leverage technology in some competitive ways.

All of this is your business.

# UNDERSTANDING EMERGING TECHNOLOGY

AI's the focus here, but remember that AI lives in a larger technology world. You need to track AI's position on the list and the role it plays as a partner with the other technologies. No, this is not another "assignment" for you, but it's important that you understand that AI's not the only technology available to solve your company's problems.

Executive understanding of technology is often incomplete and sometimes even dangerous to the pursuit of corporate strategies. If you doubt this, ask yourself how many executives understand "technology" as well as they understand sales, finance, marketing and human resources.

Technology literacy requires you to understand the range of existing and emerging technologies and how they might impact your business processes, models and strategies. This understanding is not at the engineering level or how a computer scientist might explain AI and ML, but at the contextual and purposeful levels.

The backdrop is not encouraging. Huge gaps about all things digital remain among executives and even CIOs and CTOs (McKendrick, 2021; Weill et al., 2021):

> *The analysis of almost 2,000 large companies find only 7% have digitally savvy executive teams. Even more surprising, only 47% of CTOs and 45% of CIOs could be considered "digitally savvy." This percentage drops to 24% for COOs and 23% of CEOs.*

There's additional survey research and interview data about executive shortcomings and "misunderstandings" (Weill et al., 2019; Forth et al., 2020; Cheng et al., 2021; Graves, 2021; Panetta, 2016), which describe some of the ways executives *should* understand technology.

Executives should understand the relationships among emerging technologies, problems and strategy. You should be capable of "matching" technologies to problems. This means you should have the ability to reverse engineer solutions from desired strategic outcomes with realistic technology solutions. The matching process should be *proactive*: it should not be unusual for you to suggest how specific technologies could be leveraged onto specific business models and processes. You should not wait for suggestions from your teams. They should be active participants in the matching process. For example, you should be quite capable of suggesting how AI might automate parts of the recruiting or training processes. You should help suggest how augmented and virtual reality might improve your marketing strategies. *The ability to match technologies with problems should become one of your core competencies.*

No one underestimates the extraordinary range of your corporate responsibilities. Adding "technology" to your core competencies is not just another activity. Technology touches every internal and external process there is. It's not hyperbole to say that without technology you have no business, and without AI your business will suffer. But remember that AI is not the only technology that can impact your business, so you need to have some awareness of the full range of emerging technologies that can make you more competitive.

# Digital Transformation Isn't About ERP Anymore – It's About AI

# 16

## ABSTRACT

*The chapter posits that the traditional role of enterprise resource planning (ERP) systems is fundamentally challenged by rapid advancements in artificial intelligence (AI). The chapter argues that the focus of digital transformation is shifting from functional standardization and management to a broader imperative of digital automation, driven by the need for cost savings, efficiency gains and process optimization. It suggests a future where the emphasis moves away from user-centric ERP interfaces toward autonomous processes powered by intelligent bots and AI, potentially diminishing the need for extensive human interaction with these systems. The chapter questions the viability of widespread, large-scale ERP deployments and migrations, predicting a shift toward more agile and specialized automation platforms that operate independently of traditional ERP constraints.*

Not so many years ago companies defined "digital transformation" as (Wikipedia, 2025c):

> *The use of new, fast and frequently changing digital technology to solve problems. It is about transforming processes that (are) non digital or manual to digital processes.*

Companies rushed to standardize their business processes with enterprise resource planning (ERP) systems, like the formidable, almost pervasive, applications from SAP and other ERP vendors. The value proposition was – and remains – enterprise centralization, standardization and integration across internal and external business processes, cost savings and – in spite of their still largely monolithic architectures – some flexibility (compared to the chaos that existed before). Kim O'Shaughnessy says it better (2025):

> *Enterprise resource planning (ERP) systems are used by organizations looking to manage their business functions within a centralized and integrated system … ERP brings together customer management, human resources, business intelligence, financial management, inventory and supply chain capabilities into one system.*

For many companies, these capabilities were – and remain – a God-send. The basic functionality of enterprise applications can organize a company's business processes and whole business models. All good, for sure. But is this a sustainable role given what's happening with machine learning and generative AI (GenAI)? Clearly, companies will invest heavily in automaton to save money and eliminate, streamline and optimize processes. They will map and mine their business processes for maximum impact. They will do this as quickly as possible.

# DIGITAL TRANSFORMATION IS NOW DIGITAL AUTOMATION

Digital transformation today is still about organization and standardization, but it's also about automation. In fact, it will continue to be much more about automation than functional standardization. While enterprise applications vendors (like SAP) and ERP vendor enablers (like UiPath) are investing heavily in automation, the most automated companies will move past their enterprise applications to functionality that's increasingly automated outside of older application architectures. Why is this important to you? For one thing, companies will focus much more on the processes that can be automated than ones than can be "tracked" and "managed." Ideally, much of what enterprise applications "users" do will be replaced by machine learning and GenAI. The obsession with "UI" and "UX" (user interfaces and user experiences), for example, will eventually vanish altogether.

How many companies will deploy new (or migrate from existing) ERP systems over the next ten years? Not as many as did ten years ago, that's for sure. Instead, they will:

- Identify and model business problems
- Map and optimize business processes (via process mining) that identify process optimization opportunities
- Identify, collect, validate and leverage structured and unstructured data onto target business processes
- Match problems, processes, data with machine learning algorithms and GenAI
- Extend the approach to as many processes as possible

These activities are all focused on automation. Said differently, they're focused on automating – and replacing – ERP modules and processes like human resources, financial management, business intelligence and supply chain optimization. In fact, much of the internal and external business cycle can be automated. But automation extends beyond tactical goals. What are the best profitability strategies? What new markets make the most sense? How should you innovate? When you increase the range of algorithmic applications across supervised to unsupervised machine learning, you can move from tactical to strategic automation.

Just like almost everything, this will all end up in the cloud. If you haven't already, you need to fully automate in the cloud. Note that the major cloud providers – AWS, Azure, Google and IBM – have offered AI services of one kind or another for some time. Now they offer all flavors of cloud-based AI.

Companies will shift their platform thinking *from* large centralized, standardized and integrated enterprise applications *to* platforms that automate business processes and models independent of a single application. While ERP vendors rush to automate their functions, other vendors will take a very different approach. They will identify and model business problems; map and optimize business processes (via process mining) well beyond the processes embedded in ERP applications; identify, collect, validate and leverage structured and unstructured data; match problems, processes, data and machine learning algorithms; and extend the approach to as many known, new and anticipated processes as possible. They will pursue all this outside the boundaries and constraints of their ERP applications. As long as ERP-based "automation" is confined to the automation of processes embedded in the ERP application itself, the ERP world will lag behind next generation digital transformation as it transforms to digital automation. But if you look at what ERP vendors are doing, it's clear they got the message about AI loud and clear. You should too.

# Resignations and AI, Industry by Industry **17**

---

## ABSTRACT

---

*The ongoing "Great Resignation," characterized by unprecedented numbers of Americans leaving their jobs or demanding improved work conditions, presents a significant challenge for employers, particularly in human-intensive service industries like fast food and agriculture. While some employers have responded with increased wages and better working conditions, these measures have not fully stemmed the tide of resignations. The chapter argues that labor shortages and rising labor costs will act as powerful stimuli for the adoption of AI.*

Who really cares about resignations? Well, you care, because without employees – especially in the service industries – you have no customers. Some executives are responding to the walkouts with higher wages and better working conditions, a perfectly rational response to resignations. But this tactic isn't working fast enough, even as wages have increased (note that the official minimum wage in the U.S. has been $7.25 per hour since 2009).

AI's role will also increase in response to declining birth rates around the world, but especially in developed countries. The fear is that too many countries will have less people and the ones they have will be older. This is the perfect springboard to automation.

DOI:10.1201/9781003652748-20

# THE REVENGE OF AI

Those who explore the Future of Work know all about automation. It's the cornerstone of the predicted future. Timelines about the arrival of automated solutions across industries are impossible to make. But what you *can* make are predictions about how welcome automation will be across a number of industries, including the ones where the greatest resignations (and declining birth rates) are occurring – and especially in most human-intensive ones, such as fast food and agriculture, as just two examples of how industries are responding to labor shortages.

## Automation and Fast Food

Fast food restaurants are investing heavily in automation. Motivation? "Fast-food's biggest players are letting the robots right in through the front door as they seek out ways to overcome rising wages and worker shortages." As reported by Brian Sozzi (2021) in Yahoo News, McDonalds, Domino, Taco Bell, among others, reported some years ago that "automation" was – and still is – all the rage.

## Automation and Agriculture

Agriculture is one of the most aggressive targets of automation. Robotics are already having impact on the industry. Some examples (thanks to Donovan Alexander's [2023] reporting in *Interesting Engineering*) include *Ecorobotix's fully autonomous drone, Energid Citrus Picking Systems and Vision Robotics' vineyard pruner.*

# AUTOMATION EVERYWHERE

The pandemic, The Great Resignation, "quiet quitting" and declining birth rates all accelerate investments in automation. The robotic examples here are in just two areas, but automation doesn't stop there. Do we need tax preparers? Car salesmen? Loan officers? Automation has only just begun, and as more and more employees call it quits – or are never born – automated workers may take their place faster than we think. The incentives are clear. Why wouldn't Uber want to eliminate their biggest headache – drivers – with autonomous vehicles? Why wouldn't all companies want to deploy "workers" that work 24/7, never need vacations and never get sick (from viruses, at least)? Checkout clerks? Postal workers? Gas station attendants (almost gone now)? And many more.

Honeywell reports (2024) some survey results:

> *A warehouse that might typically require 2,000 workers could deploy technologies and warehouse execution software to instead operate with only 200 people ... robotic technologies directly replace labor, whether it be unloading trucks, picking orders, fulfilling orders.*

# NOW WHAT?

The pandemic, The Great Resignation and declining birth rates unleashed unanticipated new forces and created unexpected collateral damage. Business owners, shareholders and investors who want to see profitable growth will respond with a vengeance. Remember that automation happens when the die-is-cast meets the law-of-unintended-consequences.

We're here.

# AI Leadership Consensus at Your Own Risk

# 18

## ABSTRACT

*This chapter argues that while open discussion has its place, the pursuit of consensus in artificial intelligence (AI) decision-making is a recipe for stagnation and competitive disadvantage. Challenging the idealized vision of "servant leadership" and universal buy-in, this chapter asserts the critical need for decisive AI leadership. It examines the dysfunctions of consensus, including slowed decision-making, the fostering of unproductive internal divisions and the frustration arising from uninformed opinions holding sway. The chapter identifies several critical leadership traps that can derail AI initiatives, including title inflation, self-delusion, absenteeism, a lack of technical understanding, prioritizing style over substance, reliance on the wrong influencers and sheer incompetence. By explicitly addressing these pitfalls, this chapter provides a crucial guide for organizations seeking to navigate the complexities of AI adoption.*

Everyone deserves to express their opinion about artificial intelligence (AI), right? Well, actually, no. C-Suites that insist upon listening to everyone about everything all the time will get nothing done. Executives who manage by consensus usually fail. Why? How many companies have time to debate every aspect of every problem before pulling the trigger? How patient should you be as you wait to hear from everyone on a long decision-making list? Is this true for "debates" about AI? It is, and you should encourage discussion, but at the end of the day, make the call: AI is here to stay, and you need to understand and optimize it – *as quickly as possible* – before your competitors do.

DOI:10.1201/9781003652748-21

So here's a bit of AI leadership advice. It's controversial in the age of "servant-leadership," whatever that actually is. No, this is about cutting through the nonsense that surrounds all major management decisions, and, make no mistake, the decisions you make about AI are as important as they get.

# LEADING – AND LOSING – BY CONSENSUS

Leading by consensus is a popular management approach (University of Florida, 2015):

*Consensus decision-making is a process in which a group or team arrives at a decision that all can support. All members, including the leader, have an equal share or stake in the decision and have the ability to support or block the decision.*

But does it work? No, so why is it still so appealing?

*A leader's wish to avoid conflict, or to avoid being perceived as controlling, mean, or power-hungry, makes consensus building seem like a good approach. Sadly, every leader learns they must learn to tolerate making people unhappy and not being liked.*

It's amazing how many management theorists promote consensus decision-making when the risks are so great. As described by Prudy Gourguechon, there are any number of reasons why consensus decision-making fails (Gourguechon, 2022):

*It slows everything down, sometimes to the point of a standstill.*

*It easily encourages lasting splits in the ranks.*

*It makes people anxious. Imagine a military unit in combat if consensus were needed before taking an action.*

Related to anxiety is frustration where decision-makers wonder why so many colleagues have so much to say about problems about which they know so little. There's also the risk of title infringement, where leaders justify participation based on wide interpretations of their job descriptions. Finally, without clear decision-making governance, consensus decision-making creates a kind of management chaos.

# WHAT TO DO ABOUT AI

Erase any ambiguity about who's in charge of what decisions. Ambiguity will revert to consensus – which is no way to get things done. Scream often and loudly about who's in charge of what decisions. Define an open season for input, which should be short and well-defined. For example, a draft strategic plan could be released where there's a one-week call for comments. Transparency then calls for a "defense" where the reasons why some comments were accepted and some rejected are described. Never live in secrecy because secrecy undermines credibility every time, all the time. Transparency is everyone's friend and neutralizes complaints about power-hungry executives – though transparency won't always make everyone happy.

Unambiguous accountability and the power that enables it can also breed resentment, jealousy and irrational competition – especially if those with decision-making power are incompetent. Competency is the perfect antidote to consensus decision-making, just as incompetency threatens accountability, though if a company empowers lots of incompetent decision-makers, no decision-making style will work.

If your corporate culture is – and has always been – consensus-driven, the challenge is systemic. If you demand consensus decision-making then decision-making will likely remain consensus-driven. What do you do when one or both of these situations exist? Avoid challenges to your culture *or you* unless both are failing, in which case changes of all kinds will be welcomed.

There's a two-step process required here. The first is the empowerment of competent leaders and the second is the death of consensus decision-making. Conversely, if leadership is incompetent, authority decision-making could create far more problems than it solves.

# AI LEADERSHIP CHALLENGES

As suggested, AI leadership requires some special skills, not the least of which is decisiveness and the avoidance of leadership consensus. This breaks with traditional leadership "theories." There are other AI leadership traps.

The premise here is that AI requires a different flavor of leadership because of its potential impact and the speed with which it's developing. Let's look at some of the problems that AI leadership – all leadership, in fact – should avoid.

# Title Problems

One of the phenomenons I've observed is the mismatching of capabilities with requirements. Many leaders are hired because they have things in common with members of the search team, sell emotional connections or convince people they will grow into the title – not because their experience clearly qualifies them for the job. Sometimes they're hired because they pose no threat to existing leadership, which, by definition, makes them lesser candidates. Mismatching – along with "friendship" – is perhaps the best explanation for bad leadership. Leaders are hired because of "features" that often have nothing to do with leadership requirements. Often the "heir apparent" is designated well in advance. How does *that* practice work? Since everyone knows who the next leader will be, why are there so few challenges to the heirs who are – as Texans like to say – "all hat, no cattle?"

Another phenomenon is how quickly everyone adapts to bad leaders – not to their incompetence – but to the trappings of their titles. Instead of calling them out for their incompetence, which is almost immediately discovered, they search creatively for ways to serve their own vested interests. Truth-telling is way too rare. Work-arounds are everywhere. Are there geniuses of dysfunctional playgrounds? You bet there are. AI leadership should not fall victim to these frequent worst practices. All good and all too frequent. But if you hire the wrong AI leaders for the wrong reasons, your AI initiatives will fail.

# Self-Delusion

Perhaps the strongest quality of bad leaders is their ability to delude themselves about their capabilities. I've been told by leadership coaches and psychologists that a little self-delusion is actually a necessary leadership quality, as long as it doesn't suffocate all of the other qualities. I've known many leaders who really believe they're good at their jobs – as products fail, the stock falls, talent leaves and quiet-quitting becomes the preferred survival strategy among their employees. The amount of disdain for these leaders is incredible. Leader-mocking is a favorite pastime. But the leaders refuse to look in the mirror, and no one has the courage or professionalism – usually for financial reasons – to tell them they're horrible leaders and it's time to leave. Leadership coups are few and far between. Even interventions are rare – as the ship sinks. Fiduciary responsibleness is muddled by lawyers and stock options.

If you hire delusional AI leaders, you will fail.

# Absenteeism

Many of the leaders I've known have spent more time hiding than leading. They could punt for any team in the NFL. They're incapable of making hard decisions, which by definition makes them bad leaders. They live in Hopeville, where they want problems to just disappear. I've known leaders who act as though problems don't even exist when everyone around them sees the house on fire. One of the metrics I use to assess leaders is their ability to shirk their responsibilities. Some of them have perfected shirking in unimaginable ways. They're almost invisible – which is what they want to be.

Shirking and invisibility are exactly the opposite of what you need in your AI leadership team.

# Uninformed

Many of the leaders I've known know very little about the technology that powers their companies or the products and services they sell. This is exasperating. How in the world can they lead a company that, for example, sells technology products or services when their knowledge of technology is so shallow? *This will not work for AI.*

# Style Vs Substance

I know at least fifty executives who lead with their smiles. Make no mistake, the smiles are wonderful. But they're empty suits. Many of them are articulate, superb golfers and the life of the parties they always attend. They tell jokes. They're charming. It works for them. They have a set of techniques that endears them to their teams – and protects their survival. Classic style versus substance. But it's always temporary. When the team eventually realizes that off-sites, platitudes, lunches and tweets don't define leadership, the smiles turn downward. Smiles can take them only so far. Have you ever wondered why salespersons usually only last 2–3 years? Style versus substance.

You can appoint stylists to run your AI projects or you can default to substance. If you go with substance over style, you will be breaking with the smiling crowd, but you may get some things done.

# Wrong Influencers

Bad leaders often listen to the wrong people. All leaders should know the strengths and weaknesses of their team members. They should also know how each member of their team is perceived by the larger population of their company. We've all seen all-hands meetings where exactly the wrong people stand alongside the boss, where employees just shake their heads – and credibility instantly dies. This, of course, is an extension of self-delusion, but rather than worry about the downside, there's often an unexploited upside where smart professionals are never asked what they think or what they would do. Instead, the same cronies have the ear of the boss – the same cronies who have failed to solve persistent problems. If you find yourself in a ditch, ask hard questions about how you got there. Inspect the process that got you into the ditch and who you turned to for advice. Be as objective as you can here, if you can be objective at all (since, after all, *you* may have given the cronies their seats at the table).

When it comes to AI, you must resist the sycophants and appoint professionals (and individual contributors) who are well-respected. Otherwise your AI projects will suffer the same fate as so many other projects that failed to launch.

## Incompetence

Some leaders are just plain incompetent: "they lack the qualities needed for effective action (and are) unable to function properly." Said a little differently, incompetent leaders just don't know what to do, don't know how to solve problems, don't know how to interact with humans to solve problems, run from tough problems, have no idea about precedents or best practices, or know much of anything that qualifies them for the title they hold. How many times have you been "stunned," "shocked" and "amazed" at how ineffective the leaders in your world have been? Maybe they're just incompetent.

Please do not assign incompetent people to AI projects. Everyone knows who they are. If you don't already know, just ask around.

# AI LEADERSHIP STRATEGY

AI decision-making should be purposeful, focused and timely. Consensus decision-making enables none of these things. The concentration of power is smart – so long as the concentrates are competent. Since the percentage of leaders who are clearly competent is not nearly as high as it should be (and those in charge often have little self-awareness of their inadequate skills and incompetencies), consensus decision-making is its own landmine. Is this why there's still so much of it? Does consensus decision-making provide aircover for executives unsure of their abilities? Does consensus decision-making provide protection from huge mistakes? Yes, it does. But as suggested, it may well be that authority (or small-group) decision-making only works when leaders are competent.

Ultimately, AI decision-making effectiveness requires AI competency. But consensus decision-making restricts competency, as it protects incompetency. If you're competent, consensus decision-making is ineffective. But if you're incompetent, it may save companies from decision disasters. So why do so many management "theories" fail to identify competency as the ultimate driver of success?

Look, there's urgency here. The capabilities of AI, machine learning and generative AI are exploding and will continue to explode probably forever. No kidding, this is the ultimate transformative technology. The recommendation here is to avoid consensus decision-making and all of the "features" that come with it. You just don't have the time to host debates, seminars or colloquia or deal with "leaders" who were never leaders to begin with. You must make decisions, so start learning and playing with AI regardless of the feathers you ruffle.

# Don't Worry About Affective Computing (or the Singularity)

# 19

## ABSTRACT

*This chapter questions the fundamental assumptions underlying emotion recognition by machines. The chapter explores the inherent difficulties in accurately correlating external signals with specific emotions and the potential for misinterpretation and flawed responses. Ultimately this chapter argues that the pursuit of truly feeling machines remains highly speculative. The chapter also touches upon anxieties surrounding "The Singularity."*

The aspirational power of artificial intelligence (AI), machine learning and generative AI to "think" and "feel" like humans is beyond computational reach. The irony, of course, is that we're surrounded by emotional leaders who make all kinds of mistakes – including embedding algorithmic biases – precisely because they're emotional. Even if we could do it, the last thing we need are machines that mimic human emotions or try to interpret what their human partners are feeling and react according to their interpretation of emotional situations. More to the point, we can never do this with the certainty of micro-dosing weeds, giving or denying loans or picking ripe apples – activities doing quite well in the well-bounded world of supervised learning. Or can we?

DOI:10.1201/9781003652748-22

# AFFECTIVE COMPUTING

What are we talking about here (Wikipedia, 2025a):

> *Affective computing is the study and development of systems and devices that can recognize, interpret, process, and simulate human affects. It is an interdisciplinary field spanning computer science, psychology, and cognitive science ... one of the motivations for the research is the ability to give machines emotional intelligence, including to simulate empathy. The machine should interpret the emotional state of humans and adapt its behavior to them, giving an appropriate response to those emotions.*

Let's see if we have this right (Cooney, et al., 2018):

> *Affective computing (is) emotion recognition, and sentiment analysis ... to improve people's well-being ... through awareness of people's emotions. Emotions can be recognized, with varying degrees of accuracy, from various signals, including facial expressions, gestures, and voices, using wearables or remote sensors.*

Can this really be done? I mean do our facial expressions convey definable emotions? What about all those times when someone looks at you and asks, "what are you thinking about?," and you respond, "I have no idea," because you really don't. Is this at all like lie detectors, where if you react to something behaviorally by squinting or rolling your eyes, the emotion behind these gestures will be interpreted by an affective machine? Will it be the same for sighing, sweating, coughing or taking too many deep breaths in what WebMD says is too short a period of time? Who's the domain expert that determines the linkage among behavior, the emotions it represents and the "correct" response? Can you correlate with confidence?

# NOT SO FAST

Someone – Lisa Feldman-Barrett (2021) – has already suggested that "we don't understand how emotions work." She explains why we often get it wrong:

> *Companies claim to have machine learning algorithms to detect emotion from smiles and scowls, but they're detecting muscle movements,*

*not the emotional meaning of those movements in context ... scowling isn't the universal expression of anger, just one expression among many.*

She also suggests that, for example, "we don't all make the same expressions when we're sad." "She argues that many of the key beliefs we have about emotions are wrong. It's not true that we all feel the same things, that anyone can 'read' other people's faces, and it's not true that emotions are things that happen to us."

When asked the following (Chen, 2017):

*I'm curious what all this means for affective computing, or the startups that try to analyze your facial expression to figure out how you're feeling. Does this mean their research is futile?*

Dr. Barrett replied:

*As they are currently pursuing it, most companies are going to fail. If people use the classical view to guide the development of their technology – if you're trying to build software or technology to identify scowls or frowns and pouts and so on and assume that means anger, good luck.*

## MAYBE "GOOD" APPLICATIONS?

Bernard Marr (2016) describes some "good" outcomes:

*E-learning programs could automatically detect when the learner was having difficulty and offer additional explanations or information.*

*In-car technology that can sense when you're drowsy or distracted, and can contact emergency services or a friend or family member in an emergency situation.*

## WORRY WITHOUT PURPOSE

Is affective computing likely to succeed or fail? The real question should focus on the contribution affective computing can make to human-computer interaction as the gap between humans and machines narrows. Wearables with IoT are already performing affective tasks along with health monitors of all kinds. Affective computing companies – and there are lots of them – expect to generate business from watching and feeling, but the savvy ones will do so on a continuum of complexity and reliability. Some affective computing applications will yield useful results especially when multiple "sensors" are combined, and especially when correlations can be validated. Marketing, healthcare, customer service, transportation and other applications can be useful. Real-time sensor data collection is best, especially for the application domains listed above. Some of these applications will require some tweaking – and permissions – since affective computing invades every partner's privacy in too many ways to count.

So we've arrived at the beginning. As always with emerging technology, it depends upon how you see things and the applications that are targeted. Those who control definitions, however, might want to dilute the definition of affective computing just to be sure it doesn't feel too weird.

# WORRY EVEN LESS ABOUT "THE SINGULARITY"

This might be a good time – since we're talking about connections between smart machines and human behavior – to take a quick look at everyone's favorite AI demon, "The Singularity," which is defined by our friends at Wikipedia (2025b):

> *The technological singularity – or simply the singularity – is a hypothetical point in time at which technological growth becomes uncontrollable and irreversible, resulting in unforeseeable changes to human civilization. According to the most popular version of the singularity hypothesis, called intelligence explosion, an upgradable intelligent agent will eventually enter a runaway reaction of self-improvement cycles, each new and more intelligent generation appearing more and more rapidly, causing an explosion in intelligence and resulting in a powerful superintelligence that qualitatively far surpasses all human intelligence.*

Predictions about the arrival of this event vary, of course, but I have another perspective, which essentially welcomes super-intelligence into our worlds. Is it horrific and threatening when the best doctors are machines, or when machines provide universal healthcare (in the U.S.), or when drug discoveries and genomic research are enabled by really smart machines? Of course, these "machines" can be abused, but if the singularitists are right then the machines will self-correct – as superior intellects will do – and avoid some of the major disasters that have plagued humans for centuries. Without getting overly philosophical, why shouldn't humans welcome and partner with expanded intelligence regardless of its form? Especially when, according to subscribers to the singularity, we have no choice. So until the machine intelligence explosion occurs, perhaps we should worry more about the explosions that have killed millions of humans over the years and look to smart machines to help us live longer and better lives. If they can free us from tedium, help us stay healthier and propel us toward a safer future, I don't think we should fear them at least until they become as lethal as the "intelligence" we face today.

The counterpoint? Is it just too ironic to ask "AI" if Artificial Super Intelligence (ASI) will kill us? I asked, and here's what I got:

*Reasons for Concern*

> Loss of Control: This is perhaps the most significant fear. If an ASI emerges that is far more intelligent than humans, it might optimize for goals that are not aligned with human values or even our survival. Even if its initial programming seems benign, its superintelligence could lead it to find unexpected or radical ways to achieve its objectives, potentially at humanity's expense.
>
> Existential Risk: ASI could pose an existential threat to humanity, leading to our extinction or irreversible subjugation. This could happen through various means, such as unintended consequences, direct conflict if its goals clash with ours or simply by viewing humanity as an obstacle or inefficient use of resources.
>
> Unpredictability: The Singularity implies a future beyond our current comprehension. We cannot truly predict the actions or motivations of an intelligence vastly superior to our own, making it inherently unsettling.
>
> Job Displacement and Economic Disruption: While not an existential threat, the path to Singularity could involve massive automation, leading to widespread job displacement and economic inequality on an unprecedented scale, causing social unrest.
>
> Weaponization: An ASI, or even an AI leading up to it, could be weaponized by malicious actors, leading to devastating consequences.
>
> Ethical and Moral Ambiguity: How do we instill human ethics and morals into a superintelligence, especially when there's no universal agreement on what those even are?

*Reasons for Optimism*

> Solving Grand Challenges: ASI could rapidly solve humanity's most pressing problems, such as climate change, disease (including aging), poverty and resource scarcity. It could lead to unprecedented scientific breakthroughs and technological advancements.
>
> Enhanced Human Capabilities: Instead of replacing us, AI could augment human intelligence and capabilities, leading to "human-AI integration." This could involve brain-computer interfaces, advanced prosthetics and cognitive enhancements, blurring the lines between human and machine.
>
> Abundance and Utopia: If managed correctly, the Singularity could lead to a post-scarcity world where basic needs are met and humans are freed from mundane labor, allowing us to pursue creative, intellectual and fulfilling endeavors.
>
> New Frontiers of Knowledge: ASI could unlock secrets of the universe that are currently beyond our grasp, expanding our understanding of reality in profound ways.

You decide which perspective makes the most sense. I can't wait for ASI. I think we need all the help we can get. No? Take a good look around.

# AI Will Fuel Huge Cloud Services with Massive Ecosystems

20

---

## ABSTRACT

*This chapter argues that the inevitable next phase in the evolution of artificial intelligence (AI), machine learning and generative AI (GenAI) is their full integration into the cloud, mirroring the established models of enterprise software like ERP, CRM and DBMS. The major cloud providers are already engaged in an AI arms race, developing, partnering or acquiring capabilities to deliver these services at scale. This will subsequently foster robust ecosystems, complete with vendors, consultants and talent pools, much like the infrastructure and application ecosystems that currently underpin global commerce. While the full productization of machine learning and GenAI is still underway, the chapter posits a 2–3 year timeframe for widespread adoption, driven by demonstrable ROI-, OKR-, KPI- and CMM-documented use cases across various business functions and industries. The core of the chapter focuses on how organizations can prepare for this inevitable shift by proactively identifying and analyzing business processes within key areas like marketing and human resources ripe for AI implementation.*

DOI:10.1201/9781003652748-23

Large language models (LLMs) are everywhere. They do everything. They scare everyone – or at least some of us. Now what? They will become GenAI-as-a-Service cloud "products" in exactly the same way that all "as-a-service" products and services are offered. The major cloud providers (Zhang, 2024) – "Amazon Web Services (AWS), Microsoft Azure, Google Cloud Platform (GCP), Alibaba Cloud, Oracle Cloud, IBM Cloud (Kyndryl), Tencent Cloud, OVHcloud, DigitalOcean, and Linode (owned by Akamai)" – will all develop, partner with or acquire their generative AI (GenAI) capabilities and offer them as services. There will also be ecosystems around all of these tools exactly the same way ecosystems exist around all of the major enterprise infrastructures and applications that power every company on the planet. Google, AWS, IBM, Microsoft and Oracle are all in this race.

So let's look at GenAI platforms and tools like they were ERP, CRM or DBMS platforms or tools, and how you should make decisions about what tool to use, how to use them and how to apply them to real problems.

## ARE WE THERE YET?

No, we're not. Will we get there? Absolutely. The productization of machine learning and GenAI is well underway. Access to premium/business accounts is step one. Once the dust settles on this first wave of artificial intelligence (AI) applications, we'll see an arms race predicated on both capabilities *and* cost-effectiveness. ROI-, OKR-, KPI- and CMM-documented use cases will help you decide what to do. The use cases will spread across key functions and vertical industries. Companies anxious to understand how they can exploit AI will turn to these metrics and use cases to conduct internal due diligence around adoption. Once that step is completed and there appears to be promise, the next steps will be taken. This, by the way, is how you should proceed.

## PREPARING FOR THE INEVITABLE

What will you do with AI when it has been fully productized and then even commoditized? The next step is to identify and describe the business functions and processes that might benefit from AI. This is not an easy process, mostly because most companies do not have process inventories or have "mined" the processes to identify the features most amenable to AI. It's also complicated because whole business models (comprising many processes) will be GenAI targets, like marketing (Twin, 2024):

> *Professionals who work in a corporation's marketing and promotion departments seek to get the attention of key potential audiences through advertising. Promotions are targeted to certain audiences and may involve celebrity endorsements, catchy phrases or slogans, mem-orable packaging or graphic designs, and overall media exposure.*

There's more:

- *Though traditional marketing is still prevalent, digital marketing now allows companies to engage in newsletter, social media, affiliate and content marketing strategies.*
- *At its core, marketing seeks to take a product or service, identify its ideal customers and draw the customers' attention to the product or service available.*

Can AI develop marketing campaigns? Can it write press releases? Can it target customers? Yes, it can. But with what quality? Can it develop quality marketing campaigns, press releases and strategic customer targeting as effectively as marketing professionals? This is the ongoing assessment that will define adoption.

Human Resources (HR)? What are *its* processes (Kenton, 2024)?

- *Finding, recruiting, screening, and training job applicants.*
- *Handle employee compensation, benefits, and terminations.*
- *Focus on actively advancing and improving an organization's workforce with the long-term goal of improving the organization itself.*
- *Keep up to date with laws that can affect the company and its employees.*

How will AI improve, replace, automate or reimagine HR processes? In time, pretty easily.

This drill will play out everywhere. The process/technology – in this case, AI – "matching" process will preoccupy CIOs, CTOs, CEOs, CMOs and CFOs – and all of the chiefs – pretty much forever, as will the process/technology matching process with other emerging technologies.

What else? You obviously need to track AI very, very closely – including what your competitors are doing with the technology. Since the technology will grow beyond Moore's Law, companies might consider creating Task Forces and even Centers of Excellence to track AI and its application potential. Chief AI Officers? Maybe, if you have room for another Chief.

# CLOUDS AND ECOSYSTEMS

All of the cloud providers will enable the above steps. There will also be an AI ecosystem, which will consist of a (Talin, 2024):

*Network of interconnected digital technologies, platforms, and services that interact with each other to create value for businesses and consumers.*

Ecosystems also include an array of vendors constantly improving their products and services, as well as new entrants seeking to disrupt the incumbents.

Consultants will offer advice around multi-LLM management, LLM security, prompt engineering and how to avoid (or at least identify) LMM "hallucination." No doubt the consultancies will create other GenAI services they can sell.

Like all new technology ecosystems, this one will suffer from talent shortages. Universities will scramble to develop new AI courses and degrees, but will lag behind what the consultancies will offer. (Curriculum committees cannot move fast enough to keep up with the field.)

# BUSINESS AS USUAL?

Despite how many pauses occur, the development of AI will proceed. It will begin as new technology, expand in the cloud (with the usual suspects) and take its seat among the major technologies that have contributed to all things digital. It will look and feel like ERP, CRM and DBMS applications, complete with its own ecosystem. The number of use cases will grow, easing everyone into the cloud.

While it's tempting to go down the "what about (cars, planes, submarines and Uber)?" path that was presented as a disruptive technological leap, AI *is* different simply because of the breadth of its application potential and its ability to grow without scheduled maintenance. It's also different because of the application opportunities.

So pay attention to Claude, ChatGPT, Gemini, Grok and all the others, and to how AI will stimulate huge cloud services with massive ecosystems – and start identifying the processes that AI can improve, automate or eliminate at your company.

# How Generative AI Owns Higher Education

# 21

## ABSTRACT

*This chapter presents a compelling use case illustrating the profound and imminent impact of artificial intelligence (AI), particularly generative AI (GenAI), on higher education. The chapter questions the unique value proposition of traditional professorial roles in an era where AI can automate significant aspects of course creation and delivery. It also analyzes the changing nature of student engagement when AI tools can easily summarize content, provide tailored tutoring and even assist with assignments. The chapter highlights the urgent need for academia to conduct a comprehensive audit of current practices and redefine core concepts like "academic engagement" in light of AI's increasing capabilities.*

Here's a case that demonstrates the full impact artificial intelligence (AI) will have on higher education. It's here because the "domain" – higher education – is a huge one and because it describes how especially generative AI (GenAI) will redefine teaching and training.

It's astonishing that most professors, administrators and even donors don't see the proverbial train barreling down the tracks, perhaps like how climate deniers cannot explain monster storms, catastrophic rainfall, floods, droughts and summer heat. Maybe it's just a repeat of the Luddite phenomenon that surrounds the adoption of all new technology. Who knows, but worse, many universities

DOI:10.1201/9781003652748-24

have actually banned GenAI, which is a naïve attempt to regulate a technology more compelling than the Internet, and in so doing have actually provided encouragement to faculty and administrators to pretend that GenAI and its children are more of a threat than a service (though the students all enjoy the service).

# PROFESSORS AND AI

As a professor of business technology, I have begun to treat AI as a willing teaching assistant only to discover that it's much closer to a partner than an assistant. I have asked Gemini and ChatGPT (and others) to develop syllabi and then compared them with my own as a way to improve my courses. Gemini and Chat have often made terrific suggestions and found materials I had missed in what I thought was an exhaustive search.

Many professors assign readings and then discuss them in class. But what if the readings were summarized and then interpreted by GenAI? What if a professor wanted a presentation generated from the readings? Regardless of the source or format, it could be summarized, interpreted and packaged for presentation without any personal touch.

With all this power, what's the unique contribution professors really make? Arguments are made all the time about how effective classroom experiences can be; that there's something special about human-to-human contact in the learning process.

Everyone likes to reassure professors that they'll always be necessary, but will they? It may be that accreditation boards will save them from what otherwise is inevitable – which is replacement along some assist/partner/replace continuum over a period of time, but no later than 2035 (Creative Medium, 2023). Gemini has already reduced their contributions to a three-minute waltz.

What happens when syllabi are easily better than anything professors could design? When, for example, will GenAI read MRIs faster and better than radiologists? Assess more accurate breast examinations? Admit/reject students to colleges and universities better, faster and more fairly? There are trends here that cannot be ignored. It's all just around the corner. Professors are not a protected species.

What about when more and more courses move online? Professors who teach online are barely there anyway, right? You think it would occur to university professors who host online courses today that they're demonstrating how unnecessary they are to the learning process. They develop syllabi, identify content, develop (or appropriate someone else's) videos, identify assignments and tests – all of which we've already demonstrated can today be enabled by

GenAI. Fully asynchronous students often have little or no human contact with actual professors. How does all that demonstrate necessity?

Avatars? Of course! Professors can become avatars and deliver lectures. It's already happening. (You can too.)

# STUDENTS AND AI

Let's take the content and the requirements of a course – the lectures, readings, research reports, websites and essay examinations – and match these activities with GenAI. First, students do not need to read or watch anything. Let's say that again: students do not need to read or watch anything. Instead, they can rely upon summarizers and converters to reduce their workload. If they choose to avoid summarizers and converters, they can hire GenAI tutors to see how well they're doing and suggest how they might improve their performance. Regardless, they no longer have to read articles, inspect web sites, immerse themselves in textbooks, write essays or take tests.

With the help of GenAI, online students actually have very little to do. Summaries of everything are easily generated, and student requirements are almost as easily satisfied. They too don't need to read or watch anything. In completely asynchronous courses, no one even checks, even if videos can determine if they've been watched. In fact, students may appear to have read and watched everything – as evidenced in the tests "they" take – when they've barely bonded with course materials.

When students have all this help, what's their role in the learning process? First, let's assume they will use all the help they can find because it's unlikely that students will reject ways to learn faster and easier. Part-time students will especially appreciate short-cuts, since they're on a different educational clock than full-time students – who will also accept the help. But it's not at all clear how learning outcomes will be measured, unless learning outcome metrics are exchanged for others, like speed/ease up to degree completion. For students, the assignment is to understand the relationship between real versus surrogacy and how "engagement" should be defined – that ends with an "A" for the course.

# ACADEMIA AND AI

Academia's response to all this has been uneven. On the one hand, universities are warning – and punishing – students who use GenAI tools to satisfy course requirements. But on the other hand, they're teaching the technology, where students are required to use GenAI to satisfy course requirements. It's pretty quiet about how it expects faculty to deal with GenAI chatbots, CustomGPTs and AI agents.

Some wide open questions: "who does what?" Another one: "why are professors compensated the way they are when their digital assistants and partners do much of the work?" And, lastly: "how can anyone measure learning outcomes when they're contrived by GenAI chatbots, CustomGPTs and AI agents?"

Higher education needs a quick audit. The roles that professors and students should play in the education process must be re-defined – and then re-invented, if not re-imagined altogether. It's essential that professors and students understand how to work with increasingly intelligent machines that will evolve from "teaching assistants," to "faculty partners" and, eventually, to "curriculum bosses," and how faculty will share – and eventually yield – decision-making and problem-solving power over time. As suggested, students will define their roles as team members where courses are taken by themselves. The educational process will be crowded, a far cry from the old teacher-student model some believe still defines the educational process.

Accreditors and credentialists must immediately rewrite the rules as GenAI becomes a major player in the educational process. It's a GenAI/faculty/student threesome now – and forever. Watch as the differences among correspondence, distance learning and online programs shrink to nothing – and the expanding role GenAI will play in the process as the regulators of correspondence, distance learning and online programs struggle with the merger. The same process will play out in the classroom, where roles will also be re-defined, re-invented and re-imagined.

The definition of "academic engagement" will have to change as the role of GenAI explodes. Universities should engage with those who accredit educational programs to push them toward defining how "engagement" and other activities should be defined as GenAI moves from assistants to partners and beyond.

# Technology, AI and Ethics

# 22

---

## ABSTRACT

*Digital technology, while offering immense benefits, presents a growing number of ethical challenges, ranging from the proliferation of "fake news" and deepfakes to the insidious nature of algorithmic bias and surveillance capitalism. This chapter delves into the inherent tension between profit generation and ethical conduct for companies operating within the digital economy, particularly those whose business models are predicated on exploiting these very threats. While acknowledging the immense profitability of less-than-ethical practices, fueled by a lack of robust government regulation and corporate governance, the chapter introduces the Ethical OS framework as a crucial analytical tool. This framework, comprising 8 key risk areas and 32 probing questions, provides a comprehensive checklist for assessing the breadth and depth of technology-enabled ethical challenges.*

As discussed in Chapter 12, digital technology is often our friend but sometimes our enemy. "Fake news," disinformation, deepfakes, assaults on privacy, algorithmic biases and surveillance capitalism – among other threats – challenge the ethics of the majority of companies, their employees and the "users" who participate in the digital economy.

The threats especially challenge the companies that make money from fake news, disinformation, deepfakes, threats, algorithmic bias and surveillance capitalism – and there are lots of them. There are also companies that repeatedly "torture" the truth for profit. Investment banks, prominent consultancies and accounting firms are frequently fined for ethical breaches of one kind or another.[1]

DOI:10.1201/9781003652748-25

While many companies publicly struggle with ethics versus profits, opportunities to generate enormous profit from less-than-ethical behavior (Facebook's 2024 revenue was $164B and its net income was a staggering $62B [Andriole, 2024]) are everywhere – and perhaps irresistible. Polluting the ethical waters is the lack of government regulation and corporate governance around these opportunities.

The Ethical OS (2018) framework developed by the Institute for the Future and the Omidyar Network's Tech and Society Solutions Lab summarizes the ethical challenges of digital technology (Dunagan and Lipsett, 2021). The framework provides a checklist for assessing ethical risks. This checklist, expressed as questions derived from eight risk areas, can be used to measure the breadth and depth of technology-enabled ethical challenges. It's proposed here as an analytical framework for ethical consideration (see below).

# SCOPE OF THE PROBLEM

The example of how Meta/Facebook exploits the addictive properties of technology that results in "body shamed" teenage girls is more than just egregious (Haidt, 2021). Unfortunately, it's just one example of where companies cross ethical lines. Netflix's *The Great Hack* describes the conversion of data into pure propaganda. The documentary describes Cambridge Analytica's and Facebook's role in the UK's Brexit campaign and the elections of Ted Cruz and Donald Trump. The documentary also looks at the role that Cambridge Analytica played in a campaign in Trinidad and Tobago where citizens were encouraged *not* to vote.

*The Great Hack* describes how analytics can be used to manipulate behavior around major national and international events from data provided willingly by anyone who lives even a small digital life. Inference capabilities are so sophisticated that the leap from predictive to prescriptive analytics is now short: decreasing amounts of data enable inferences – and therefore manipulation. This is a pervasive ethical problem.

*The Great Hack* dances around regulatory challenges. But given the trends in digital surveillance and the ongoing assault on truth and privacy, can regulation be avoided? At the same time, it's challenging to balance free speech against regulations intended to police, restrict or eliminate posts, blogs and tweets on social and other media platforms that harm society.

Technologies like machine learning and generative AI can help a lot, but here too we see good-versus-bad artificial intelligence (AI) everywhere. ChatGPT and all of the chatbots changed the game once again. Is propaganda and manipulation inevitable? How many times have we felt misled by an advertisement? Sometimes fines are assessed, but the fines tend to be small, barely publicized and a tiny percentage of the offending company's annual revenue.

The Ethical OS framework summarizes the ethical challenges in 8 risk areas and 32 questions which together present an analytical framework for consideration (Dunagan and Lipsett, 2021).

# ETHICAL OS RISK AREAS AND QUESTIONS

Here are the risk areas and questions:

"Risk Area 1: Truth, Disinformation and Propaganda
1. What type of data do users expect you to accurately share, measure or collect?
2. How could bad actors use your tech to subvert or attack the truth? What could potentially become the equivalent of fake news, bots or deepfake videos on your platform?
3. How could someone use this technology to undermine trust in established social institutions, like media, medicine, democracy or science?
4. Could your tech be used to generate or spread misinformation to create political distrust or social unrest?

"Risk Area 2: Addiction and the Dopamine Economy
5. Does the business model behind your chosen technology benefit from maximizing user attention and engagement – i.e., the more, the better? If so, is that good for the mental, physical or social health of the people who use it? What might not be good about it?
6. What does "extreme" use, addiction or unhealthy engagement with your tech look like?
7. What does "moderate" use or healthy engagement look like? How could you design a system that encourages moderate use?

"Risk Area 3: Surveillance State
8. How might a government or military body utilize this technology to increase its capacity to surveil or otherwise infringe upon the rights of its citizens?

9. What could governments do with the data you're collecting about users if they were granted access to it or if they legally required or subpoenaed access to it?

10. Who, besides government or military, might use the tools and data you're creating to increase surveillance of targeted individuals? Whom would they track and why – and do you want your tech to be used in this way?

"Risk Area 4: Data Control and Monetization

11. Do your users have the right and ability to access the data you have collected about them?

12. If you profit from the use or sale of user data, do your users share in that profit?

13. What options would you consider for giving users the right to share profits on their own data?

14. What could bad actors do with this data if they had access to it?

15. What is the worst thing someone could do with this data if it were stolen or leaked?

"Risk Area 5: Implicit Trust and User Understanding

16. Does your technology do anything your users don't know about, or would probably be surprised to find out about?

17. Are all users treated equally? If not, do your algorithms and predictive technologies prioritize certain information or set prices or access differently for different users?

"Risk Area 6: Economic and Asset Inequalities

18. Who will have access to this technology and who won't?

19. Will people or communities who don't have access to this technology suffer a setback compared to those who do?

20. What new differences will there be between the "haves" and "have-nots" of this technology?

21. If you are reducing human employment, how might that impact overall economic well-being and social stability?

"Risk Area 7: Machine Ethics and Algorithmic Biases

22. Does this technology make use of deep data sets and machine learning?

23. If so, are there gaps or historical biases in the data that might bias the technology?

24. Have you seen instances of personal or individual bias enter into your product's algorithms?

25. Is the technology reinforcing or amplifying existing bias?
26. Is there a lack of diversity among the people responsible for the design of the technology?
27. Are your algorithms transparent to the people impacted by them? Is there any recourse for people who feel they have been incorrectly or unfairly assessed?

"Risk Area 8: Hateful and Criminal Actors
28. How could someone use your technology to bully, stalk or harass other people?
29. What new kinds of ransomware, theft, financial crimes, fraud or other illegal activity could potentially arise in or around your tech?
30. How could organized hate groups use your technology to spread hate, recruit or discriminate against others?
31. What does organized hate look like on your platform or community or users?
32. What are the risks of your technology being weaponized?"

The answers to these questions are ethical metrics. If you're concerned about the ethical impact of your products and services, the questions should help – or make you aware of some uncomfortable things. They can also provide some insight into your competitors' products and services.

AI raises all sorts of red flags since its largely opaque algorithms are making decisions about life, death, happiness, winners, losers, admissions to colleges, loans and even which start-up investments venture capitalists (VCs) should make. What about the storage of genomes? Or facial recognition software which we know often fails to correctly identify the faces of people of color? Will autonomous vehicles always recognize images (of people versus telephone poles) correctly?

# POWERFUL INCENTIVES

Companies rely upon nefarious – and, in too many cases, unethical – business models to make money with digital technology. This is the dark side of digital progress and AI. Very few of us think about the business models of these companies except that they provide capabilities and content for "free." We seldom acknowledge that these platforms are prodigious profit engines unto themselves.

Many business models rely upon misinformation, disinformation, invasions of privacy, the distortion of financial information, disingenuous marketing campaigns – and more – to acquire and monetize customers. While this is not to indict every business model, it is to unequivocally state that digital technology has improved the ability of corporations to behave badly, especially as more and more transactions move online.

If we fast-forward just five years, the world will be approaching "all-digital" status, where "data" will be available for analytics-of-the-best-and-worst kind. Unless there are serious regulatory policies and self-administered (compliance-based) corporate governance, there's every likelihood that "business" will become a free-for-all where customers and clients will be at the mercy of how corporations manipulate their behavior with data collected from the very transactions that make them "digital."

Already the majority of data generated every day is unstructured, which is precisely the kind of data (especially when combined with structured data) companies use to get to know everyone. AI, machine learning and generative AI are plowing through this data to profile every aspect of everyone's lives. Surveillance-based transactions now dominate many vertical industries. But beyond the evolution of digital transaction processing, nearly all business models already have elements of "surveillance capitalism" (Zuboff, 2019).

# EXPLAINABLE AI (XAI)

One of the ways you might open the door for "inspection" of your AI-enabled processes, products and services is to adhere to XAI, which according to the bots is pretty simple:

> Explainable AI (XAI) focuses on making the inner workings and decision-making processes of AI systems more understandable to humans. It aims to create transparent and trustworthy AI models by providing explanations for their predictions and actions. This is crucial in fields like healthcare and finance where understanding the reasoning behind an AI's decision is essential.

How does XAI work?
XAI employs various techniques to make AI models more transparent and understandable. These include:

- **Feature Attributions:** Identifying the most important input features that contributed to a specific prediction.

- **Example-Based Explanations:** Providing examples of similar inputs and their corresponding outputs to explain a model's behavior.
- **Knowledge Graphs:** Incorporating structured knowledge to provide more context and reasoning for AI decisions.
- **Decision Trees and Other Interpretable Models:** Building models that are inherently easier to understand.
- **Post-Hoc Explanations:** Explaining the behavior of a complex model after it has been trained, such as by using LIME (Local Interpretable Model-agnostic Explanations) or SHAP (SHapley Additive exPlanations).

# XAI BENEFITS?

- Improved Trust and Confidence: XAI helps users understand and trust AI models, leading to wider adoption of AI in various sectors.
- Enhanced Decision-Making: By providing insights into how AI models make decisions, XAI enables users to make more informed decisions and improve their own work.
- Reduced Bias and Fairness: XAI helps identify and mitigate biases in AI models, ensuring that they are fair and equitable in their decision-making.
- Faster Debugging and Model Improvement: By understanding the inner workings of AI models, developers can more easily identify and fix errors, leading to improved model performance.
- Increased Transparency and Accountability: XAI ensures that AI systems are transparent and accountable, building confidence in their reliability and fairness.

# ETHICAL TESTS

You should read the questions and consider some answers. You should look at your policies, products and services to determine if they "do no harm," or if they do, in fact, harm some employees, customers or clients or anyone in your professional orbit. You should also explore the role that XAI plays in your AI solutions. Open is better than closed – unless there's some reason why you want to keep things closed.

# NOTE

1  See *"Banks Worldwide Amass $15B in Fines in 2020, U.S. Banks Account for 73%."* One of the most famous examples of questionable accounting practices is PWC's "accounting" of AIG prior to the 2007–2008 global financial meltdown. PWC eventually paid nearly $100M for its role in the meltdown. McKinsey paid nearly $600,000,000 for its role in the opioid crisis. One investigator bluntly declared that "McKinsey's Business Model Is Unethical."

# PART IV

# Conclusions

# Should Machines Replace Us All?

# 23

## ABSTRACT

*This chapter confronts resistance to the widespread adoption of artificial intelligence (AI), machine learning (ML) and generative AI (GenAI), despite their demonstrated and potential superiority over human performance in numerous domains. It questions the fears that prevent the aggressive adoption of automation, particularly in areas plagued by human error, inefficiency and inherent biases. The chapter provides compelling evidence of AI's capabilities in fields like taxation, healthcare, law, finance and even warfare, and the chapter argues that the reluctance to deploy these technologies more broadly is often rooted in vested interests, outdated processes and a lack of urgency rather than the limitations of the technology itself.*

I have no idea what's taking so long. Nor should you. There are all kinds of areas where machines perform better than humans – and lots more in the queue if we only give them a chance to show us what they can do. Why are we so afraid of smart machines? Why aren't we – *you* – screaming to be replaced? Or do we like doing taxes, buying insurance, misdiagnosing illnesses or losing and filing – everything? Or is it ultimately about the jobs that will be eliminated? Or politics? Or corporate cultures? Or ignorance? You should think about questions like these that apply to your business. What can machines do better than your team? What are you waiting for?

From your perspective, this should feel a little weird. On the one hand, the message here is to exploit artificial intelligence (AI), machine learning (ML) and generative AI (GenAI) every way you can to reduce costs and increase

DOI:10.1201/9781003652748-27

revenue. One of the goals is to do all this with less people. But the "management" of AI should be in your hands and in the hands of your executive colleagues. On the other hand, the message is to replace as many people as possible – including your colleagues and maybe even you – or, easily, a lot of the things you do all day.

# LET'S STIPULATE

First, let's stipulate that not all problems can be solved with AI and ML, though the line is blurring more every day. But let's also stipulate that problems that are repetitious in well-bounded areas are tailor-made for automation. As an example, income taxes are a perfect candidate (Andriole, 2023):

*Machine learning (ML) is killing all sorts of processes and entire busi-ness models. Areas like tax planning, preparation, reporting and documentation that are well-bounded and deductive – what those in AI call "narrow AI" – are ready for supervised machine learning. What's taking so long? Everything's already digital. Your personal taxes require preparation, submission and calculation, all pretty easy for smart machines (that don't need to be all that smart to do your taxes).*

# HELP WANTED IS ALREADY HERE

So what can machines do better than humans?
Healthcare is ready and able, but not so willing. How about this (Ghosh, 2018):

*Researchers ... have developed artificial intelligence (AI) that can diagnose scans for heart disease and lung cancer. The systems will save billions of pounds by enabling the diseases to be picked up much earlier. The heart disease technology will start to be available to NHS hospitals for free this summer.*

Or this (University of Oxford, 2019):

*Technology developed using artificial intelligence (AI) could identify people at high risk of a fatal heart attack at least five years before it strikes, according to new research funded by the British Heart Founda-tion (BHF).*

There's so much more here – like medical imaging, diagnosis, drug discovery, radiation treatment and genomics, among many other areas. We should select and deploy the ones with the greatest impact and lowest cost – now.

The legal profession (LawGeez, 2018):

*Twenty US-trained lawyers ... were asked to issue-spot legal issues in five standard NDAs. They competed against a LawGeex AI system ... trained on tens of thousands of contracts ... the LawGeex Artificial Intelligence achieved an average 94% accuracy rate, ahead of the lawyers who achieved an average rate of 85%.*

Finance (Spark, 2019):

*One of the models allowed for a 73% return on investment annually from 1992 to 2015, taking into account transaction costs. This compares with a real market return of 9% per year. Profits were particularly high during the market shocks of 2000 (a 545% yield) and 2008 (a 681% yield).*

War (Lee, 2021):

*Well, we already know that drones are often the weapons of choice in many situations. We also know that robots are being groomed to replace human soldiers. Tacticians and strategists will also be automated. You name it.*

Other tasks?

How about all of the menial tasks, like those conducted by CSRs, data entry, reading, translation, phone management, manufacturing, retail, security, employee onboarding and all forms of transportation (note that the *Los Angeles Times* predicts that "self-driving trucks could replace 1.7 million American truckers in the next ten years")? It's not "likely" *but necessary* that machines solve our expertise and employment problems.

# WHY NOT?

In many areas – *not every area* – machines are smarter and faster than humans. They're also cost-effective – and they don't complain or take vacations – and they're fine with danger. Mostly good, right? (We should assess the ethics around autonomous weaponry before and after drones hit and miss their targets.)

So what's wrong? What's slowing all this down? When we look at performance data where machines clearly outperform humans, we must wonder why deployment has been so slow, even avoided. As I argued in the tax filing example, there's a multi-billion-dollar tax preparation industry that stands in the way of the automation that many countries already enjoy. There are also legitimate testing- and validation-related reasons for cautious deployment, as well as legal issues, such as liability when, for example, autonomous vehicles malfunction. But perhaps the biggest problem is that we're not nearly as desperate for help as we should be, and we're not that interested in how to replace ourselves with machines that are smarter, faster, cheaper and better than we are. Instead, we're worried and threatened. But in time, the machines will win. You know this. Everyone knows this. You need to prepare for this inevitable outcome. Just think about all the money you will save.

# FIVE IN THE KILL ZONE

If you're in one of the five industries discussed below, you should already know your company is in the kill zone. You know that technology will eventually maim and kill your industry, though you may be in public denial – like the book, CD, music and taxi industries were for years before the death they all knew was inevitable. Protecting revenue streams – even if they're dying – is a form of dystopia well-constructed by those who manage the death of business models for a living. There's really good money in death – that's for sure. But eventually the revenue stream ends and the business model dies. Is yours on the list? Or close to it?

So here's what's coming next. Actually, it's already here. All we have to do is see it.

## Insurance

The insurance industry has already been attacked by digital agents, but the digital army is now poised for a takeover. Most millennials and Zippies (GenZers) do not use human home, auto and life insurance agents (Narciso, 2015):

> *Instead of working with local agents to find the right coverage, 67% of millennials are purchasing directly from insurance companies, leaving agents out of the picture.*

Why in the world would anyone with a computer or smartphone make an appointment with a human insurance agent and physically travel to an office? Millennials and GenZ buyers seldom do.

Agents are paid conduits for insurance companies who use them as sales channels. They're willing to compensate agents who bring them business, but as buying patterns change, the value agents bring to insurance carriers will fall. More importantly, the value that agents bring to their customers is actually hard to define, especially since they make no coverage rules and essentially tell customers what's covered, what's not and how they should follow the carriers' rules. Agents have no financial incentive to challenge carriers on behalf of their clients. They're therefore not real client advocates. So-called independent agents are also stuck in the buttered-bread syndrome. If present trends continue, insurance agents will disappear around about the same time we bury the last baby boomers.

## Realtors

This industry is also under attack from companies like OpenListings and the larger "for-sale-by-owner" (FSBO) community. But the traditional players have some powerful friends that lobby endlessly to keep their hold on how real estate is bought and sold. There are so many hands in the typical transaction that it's impossible to even identify all of the financial vested interests in real estate transactions – which makes the industry difficult to attack. Listen to this POV (Kasanoff, 2014):

> *95% of a broker's role could be handled better by well-designed technology systems ... one thing keeps the broker's role alive today: the regulations that govern the real estate industry. Once upon a time they might have been designed to protect consumers, but today they mainly protect realtors.*

The disintermediation of real estate agents is more complicated than forcing cab drivers off the road – but it's inevitable. The buying and selling of property is a giant revenue stream for millions of players who all wet their beaks the second a transaction closes. There are regulatory constraints that make it difficult to disrupt the industry, but with the size of the revenue stream in play it's only a matter of time and initiative. Give it a decade.

## Banks

I have no idea why there are physical banks, human tellers or what we carry around as money. Do you? According to Brett King, the founder of Moven (as reported by Eric Rosenbaum [2015]):

*The biggest banks in the world in 2025 will be technology companies, and banks that grew through branch acquisitions in the '80s and '90s, that grew by physical bank presence, will have a real problem.*

The trends are clear:

*Since 2011, 700 million global consumers have begun banking on their phone. The U.S. bank branch model, which peaks at a total of roughly 95,000 branches, is now down to 86,000 branches.*

Money is also disappearing. Way back in 2012, Jacey Fortin reported that:

*In Sweden, monetary transactions made with physical cash are down to three percent of the national economy ... in most Swedish cities, public buses don't accept cash; tickets are prepaid or purchased with a cell phone text message.*

Merryn Somerset Webb reported that Denmark – so long ago! – quickly followed (Webb, 2015):

*The Danish government is concerned that cash puts too many 'administrative and financial burdens' on shops and that it acts as a drag on GDP growth. So, as part of a wide group of proposals to boost economic growth, it is to allow shops to stop taking cash.*

The U.S. lags of course, but it's only a matter of time and money – especially because of the control that cashless transactions provide governments and the financial gains banks accrue from closing their branches and going cashless.

Cashlessness is already happening with cryptocurrency, credit cards, debit cards, Venmo, digital wallets – you name it – especially with GenZ. Some years ago, The Pew Research Center told us that the percentage of cashless versus cash transactions was skyrocketing (Faverio, 2022).

# Professionals

There's no need for so many physical, organic, living, breathing professionals in the digital era. Expertise defined around "rules" can be automated and distributed at the touch of a key, a verbal command or a reasonably intelligent assistant. Automated reasoning will replace many lawyers, doctors, accountants, professors and engineers.

But it's not just knowledge-based professions that are at risk. Manufacturing, production and transactional professions are also at risk. According to NPR research as reported by Ben Snyder (2015):

> *Telemarketers' jobs have the highest chance of being automated ... other positions with huge potential for being overtaken by robots? Cashiers, tellers and drivers, among others, according to this new NPR interactive.*

This means that technology will disrupt knowledge- *and* production-based professions and the fields that prepare and maintain these professionals. Note that trickle-down disruption will be much more impactful than first-order disruption.

## Politics

Social media represents the tip of the political iceberg. Every time Donald Trump or Alexandria Ocasio-Cortez tweet something, and every time someone responds, there's someone in the media or academia that notes the importance of digital politics. But the long-term impact that digital technology will have on politics will be profound – and always controversial. Imagine, for example, how registration/voting by phone would affect voter registration and election outcomes. All of the discussions about voter registration and voter rights would disappear – which is why there's a major clash coming between digital technology and democratic politics.

Voting with blockchain? Of course.

There are security issues that must still be resolved before universal, global Internet voting (regardless of the device used to cast the vote) becomes routine. But given the growing dependency upon digital technology in all aspects of industry and government, it's impossible to believe that security concerns will prevent the consummation of politics and technology. The real constraints are likely to be political, not technological, though technology may well become the scapegoat for objections to fully digitizing the political process. All of that said, imagine the efficiencies around immediate communications, referenda and elections. It is easily inevitable. But so is the dark side; lots of misinformation, disinformation, deepfakes and just plain lies. Fact-checking is a lost art.

# SO WHAT?

We've seen whole industries disrupted by digital technology over the past two decades. But all of that disruption combined only represents Disruption 1.0.

The five areas discussed here represent just the beginning of Disruption 2.0. Like the iPhone, there are likely to be many incarnations over time. As machines get smaller, faster, smarter and cheaper, we'll see more and more industries disrupted by digital professionals and their digital tools. The implications of continuous disruption are extensive and unpredictable. The world as we think we know it will never be, just as it never was. AI will see to it.

# PROFIT ENGINEERING

*Let's not forget that AI, ML and GenAI will unleash the greatest profit engine in history as expensive human-managed processes are replaced by cheaper and more efficient digital ones. What we've seen to date is just the beginning of how AI will transform and reinvent business. At the end of the day, you have no choices here. You must invest in AI, ML and GenAI.*

Let's start with some outcomes. AI will:

- Forever change business processes and whole business models
- Without a doubt replace thousands if not millions of jobs
- Accelerate corruption
- Make our homes and offices more efficient
- Replace teachers and medical professionals, including surgeons
- Steal and create more money than is imaginable today
- Eliminate car salespersons, tax accountants, HR officers and lawyers
- Transform – and reinvent – production, manufacturing, supply chain management and entertainment
- Enable offensive and defensive warfare
- Increase social, political and economic surveillance
- Change transportation
- Enable genetic research
- Increase misinformation and disinformation
- Increase lower-cost agricultural production
- Reduce – and worsen – climate change
- Manage water distribution
- Increase wealth and income inequality
- Enable technology oligarchies
- Challenge competitive advantage and so many other business strategies, models and processes …

There are more outcomes, of course, but this list makes the point. Remember that today many of the applications are in well-bounded areas – like accept/

reject loans – that definitely save money and increase accuracy with simple, easily trained regression models. But tomorrow's applications will broaden with algorithmic approaches far more adaptive and powerful and interfaces (like chatbots) that make the algorithms accessible to everyone. Whole new industries will be created as older ones die. Disruptive progress for sure.

## Unimaginable Cash

Let's stop here for a moment to honor the *raison d'être of all business*: profit. AI will transform, replace and automate whole industries. Those who make money from online digital retail, production, manufacturing and distribution will make killings from the profit margins digital efficiencies will deliver.

*AI will unleash the greatest profit engine in history as expensive human-managed processes are replaced by more efficient ones. While we once believed that so-called knowledge industries would be relatively free from what AI had to offer, we now know that the real targets of AI are the knowledge industries (in addition to the more industrial and operational industries). That's where the money is.*

Sometimes show horses are fabulous. GenAI is a fabulous show horse. I love it for that reason alone, and remain amazed by its abilities. But show horses can be wake-up calls as well. ChatGPT and all of the chatbots are interfaces to the ever-expanding ocean of data that GenAI uses to create. It creates descriptions, explanations, predictions and prescriptions – all through access to a widening amount of data. That – along with embedded connectivity and inference-making – is the trick. But don't think of GenAI as the "answer" or where AI was always intended to go. It's just a step toward increasing power and influence.

## Where Vs How

We're heading toward the outcomes listed above. GenAI will enable some of these outcomes. But there's more under the covers that ML and GenAI will enable. For example, some of the technology that AI will both create and exploit includes:

- Real-time data integration
- API generation and integration
- Network configurability and reconfigurability
- Adaptive cybersecurity and cyberwarfare
- Operational technology management, including cloud optimization and management

- Integrated sensor technology
- Data-as-a-service; operations-as-a-service; strategy-as-a-service
- Prescriptive analytics-as-a-service
- Automated applications development
- Maintenance and repair …

Here too there are more examples, but these make the point.

# IT'S TIME

You have a decision to make. You can assume that while the "inevitable" may be true, you still have some time before the world changes as dramatically as I've described here. This is what most executives do: they punt big decisions to future leadership. They claim there's plenty of time to think, analyze and just watch; that there's no reason to panic. In this case, they would be wrong – *you would be wrong*. It's sort of like climate change, isn't it? Some believe we have decades to address it, while others believe the time to act has already passed – which it has.

# Some Parting Thoughts

# 24

So how should you think about artificial intelligence (AI)? First and foremost, you must respect the growing power of AI, machine learning and generative AI. If you're reading this book, you already know that AI's a game-changer. You also have some sense of what you don't know and what you need to know to optimize the most important technology in a generation. If you drag your heels on this one, you will be punished in the marketplace. I don't know how else to say this, so I will say it again: you will be punished.

You need help. Your team is AI-deprived. Over time, they will get smarter, but now you have gaps – no matter how confidently they tell you that "we've got this." They don't. Nor is "AI" something you – or anyone – can learn in a week. This is not like when professors smile about how all they have to do is stay a chapter ahead of their students. AI is wide and deep and must be matched with your company's business processes and perhaps its entire business model that descends from your overall business strategy. This mixture of AI with your processes, model and strategy is essential to how you competitively leverage AI. In fact, if you don't know what you do or where you're going, you cannot tell AI what to do. This may surprise you. But if it does, it suggests that you need to step back and think about how AI – and all emerging technology – wants problems to solve, and in your case the problems are your ineffective business process, your business model and maybe even your overall business strategy.

You need more friends-with-AI. You can never have too many. Some of them can come from your team as they upskill in AI, and some can come from AI itself. Here's what I said in the Introduction to the book:

*You have some new friends these days – and forever. Lifelong friends with strange names that you may have just met. Friends like Claude, Chat, Grok, Llama, Perplexity, Copilot, Gemini and DeepSeek and a bunch of others who desperately want to be your friends, who have all been invited into this book's discussion. It's time you widened your circle of work friends. It's time you started talking directly to Claude, Gemini, ChatGPT, Llama, Perplexity, Copilot, Grok and DeepSeek and*

DOI:10.1201/9781003652748-28

*stay open to adding more friends into your circle of trust. You should
also play with their friends and the tools they all use to help you save
money and make money.*

Throughout the book, I worked with these friends. Why in the world would
I not? Why in the world would *you* not work with the smartest "people" in the
room? If you still believe you or your team know more than these new friends
then you've wasted whatever money you paid for this book. If you believe that
loan officers can outperform algorithms then you've entirely missed the point
of this whole discussion.

The book also tries to stay at the "executive" level of communication. It
makes little or no attempt to connect with the troops in the trenches. There are
countless books, articles and training courses that will help them in every area
of AI. But here the discussion is intended to get executives – senior decision-
makers like yourself – thinking about how AI can help them compete. It's full
of ideas, suggestions and recommendations, some of which may strike you as
aggressive or even insensitive. But I'm here to convey an important message: AI
will change your business, and you have no choice but to understand how it
will change your business and how you can save or make money with AI. At
the very least, you're bound to test it against your business processes. But you
need to do it quickly.

My job is to broaden your perspective about how companies succeed. AI,
machine learning and generative AI should be part of that perspective. I hope
what we did here helps.

But at the end of the day, this all hinges on your willingness to champion
AI throughout your company. You have to become a true believer. If that's too
difficult or if you have some doubts about the impact AI will have on your
company, you need to go back to the end of the line and start again. Typically
this will buy you some time – if you really think you need more time. But as
I've argued throughout this book, you really don't have much time to accept or
reject the impact AI will have on you, your company, your competitors, your
industry, your stakeholders and your investors.

Many of the applications of AI, machine learning and generative AI today
are what we might call "tactical" or "operational." Don't be fooled by these early
applications. Yes, they can improve how we onboard new employees, process
loans and deliver news – which are all important applications – but phase-two
applications will be much more strategic, which will steer companies in new
directions, develop new products and services and solve stubborn problems in real
time. As more and more tactical and operational processes become automated,
"AI" will look for higher ground – and this is where the strategic competition
starts. First-generation applications are table stakes for the strategic real game.
This book describes these table stakes and prepares you for the big game.

So the real assignment is twofold. First, it's to understand what AI is, what it can do, what you should do about it and how you should think about the whole AI phenomenon. The second assignment is to step back and re-think how "business" – especially your business – can transform itself with AI, machine learning and generative AI. For example, how will AI re-invent marketing, finance, manufacturing and human resources? How will companies compete within this re-invented world? What happens when "marketing" is automated? What's left for "marketers" to do? Will there still be marketing professionals? Of course not. Marketing will morph into something unrecognizable today – which is the second assignment. What will it be? How will companies who sell products and services reach their customers? One thing's for sure. They will not reach their customers in any way that resembles how they reach them today. How about banking? What will that look like? Does anyone know? Same assignment.

I hope you see where all this is going. Tactics first, strategy next. But "strategy" will be different as the full force of AI hits business processes and whole business models, like how Uber hit transportation and Airbnb hit travel. What's next for marketing, finance, manufacturing, human resources, travel, defense, agriculture, real estate, technology, chemicals, energy, education, entertainment, training, healthcare, media, food, financial services, tourism, pharmaceuticals, retail, telecommunications, consulting, transportation and sustainability – among other industries? One or more of these industries may be yours. What's it going to look like when it's re-imagined? Once you've completed the first assignment, you can turn to the second one.

But there's one more aspect of AI you should understand. Within a few years, AI will automate itself. This is not a threat about "The Singularity." It's a simple fact of technology life. We will, for example, not "build" agents, custom GPTs or small language models. They will be built for us. Watch this trend closely. This is not a ten-year warning. It's 5–7 at best. Let's call it the automation of automation.

The "automation of automation?" What's that, Gemini?

*The "automation of automation" refers to the next level of techno-logical advancement where AI and intelligent systems are used to design, implement, manage, and optimize other automation systems, often with minimal or no human intervention.*

*Think of it as moving from automating individual tasks to auto-mating the process of creating and managing those automations themselves.*

*The "automation of automation" promises to unlock even greater levels of efficiency, scalability, and resilience in various domains. It aims to overcome the limitations of traditional automation, which often*

*requires significant human effort for initial setup, ongoing mainten-*
*ance, and adaptation to changing conditions.*

This means that the AI "applications" your team builds today will eventually build themselves. So should you invest in the automation of automation
today? No. But the perspective is necessary to understand the trajectory of AI,
machine learning and generative AI.

This book describes how you should think about AI and the inevitable
impact AI will have on your business, your company, your career, your wealth
and your life. It's all inevitable and I hope the book has convinced you about
how AI will impact your future. At the end of the day, AI is an opportunity
that can create competitive advantage. It's time to spend some money to make
some money.

Good luck.

Call me if you ever want to talk.

# References

Alexander, D. (2023). "9 Robots That Are Invading the Agriculture Industry." *Interesting Engineering*. June.

Alvarez, G. (2024). "Gartner Top 10 Strategic Technology Trends for 2025." *The Gartner Group*. October.

Andriole, S. (2023). "Five Ways Executives Misunderstand Technology." *Communications of the ACM*. December.

Andriole, S. (2024). "The Ongoing Scourge of Social Media." *Medium*. March.

Badshah, N. (2024). "Nearly 4,000 Celebrities Found to Be Victims of Deepfake Pornography." *The Guardian*. March.

Belli, L. (2025). "What Leaders Need to Know About Auditing AI." *Harvard Business Review*. March.

Bishop, K. and Karpel, A. (2024). "CrowdStrike Issue Causes Major Outage Affecting Businesses Around the World." *CNBC*. July.

ChatGPT. (2023). https://openai.com/blog/chatgpt. *OpenAI*.

Chen, A. (2017). "Neuroscientist Lisa Feldman Barrett Explains How Emotions Are Made," *The Verge*. April.

Cheng, J.W., Frangos, C. and Groysberg, B. (2021). "Is Your C-Suite Equipped to Lead a Digital Transformation?" *Harvard Business Review*.

Cisco. (2024). "Cisco's 2024 AI Readiness Index: Urgency Rises, Readiness Falls." *Cisco News*. November.

Cooney, M., Pashami, S., Pinheiro Sant'Anna, A., Fan, Y. and Nowaczyk, S. (2018). "Pitfalls of Affective Computing: How Can the Automatic Visual Communication of Emotions Lead to Harm, and What Can Be Done to Mitigate Such Risks?" *ACM Publications*.

Cordovez, J. (2016). "If You Want Exponential Growth, Forget Linear Thinking." *Medium*. July.

Coutu, D. (2009). "Why Teams Don't Work." *Harvard Business Review*. May.

Creative Medium. (2023). "Will AI Replace College Professors." *Creative Medium*. December.

Dans, E. (2023). "Why Do We Always See New Technology as a Threat?" *Medium*. April.

deVos, K. (2024). "ASU Researchers Discuss the Implications of Deepfake." *ASU News*. June

Dunagan, J. and Lipsett, I. (2021). "A Playbook for Ethical Technology Governance: Helping Governments Anticipate and Prepare for Unintended Consequences of New Technology." *Institute for the Future*. July.

Dunham, R. (2023). "6 AI Tools That Can Help You Combat Deepfakes. *International Journalists' Network*. October.

Ellingrud, K., Sanghvi, S., Dandona, G., Madgavkar, A., Chui, M., White, O. and Hasebe, H. (2023). "Generative AI and the Future of Work in America." *McKinsey*. July.

Ethical OS. (2018). "A Guide to Anticipating the Future Impact of Today's Technology."

Faverio, M. (2022). "More Americans Are Joining the 'Cashless' Economy." *Pew Research*. October.

Forth, P., Reichert, T., de Laubier, R. and Saibal Chakraborty, S. (2020). "Flipping the Odds of Digital Transformation Success." *Boston Consulting Group.*

Fortin, J. (2012). "Sweden Going Cashless: Pros and Cons of Paper Money." *IBTimes*. March.

Fried, I. (2023). "Generative AI Is a Legal Minefield." *Axios.*

From the Interface. (2020). "How DARPA Drives Brain Machine Interface Research." *From the Interface*. November.

Future of Life Institute (2023). "Pause Giant AI Experiments: An Open Letter." *Future of Life Institute*. March.

Ghosh, P. (2018). "AI Early Diagnosis Could Save Heart and Cancer Patients." *BBC News*. January.

Gourguechon, P. (2022). "7 Reasons Why Decision-Making by Consensus Is a Bad Idea (and What To Do Instead)." *Forbes Magazine*. January.

Graham, M. M. (2024). "Deepfakes: Federal and State Regulation Aims to Curb a Growing Threat." *Thomson Reuters*. June.

Graves, D. (2021). "Today's CEOs Need Hands-On Digital Skills." *Harvard Business Review.*

Haidt, J. (2021). "The Dangerous Experiment on Teen Girls." *The Atlantic.*

Hiskey, M. (2024). "The Avatar as Instructor." *AACSB*. April.

Hone. (2025). "What Is An Induvial Contributor?" *Honehq.*

Honeywell. (2024). "Why Companies Say Automation Is a Top Goal." *Honeywell.*

Hutchins, S.F. and Botkin, R.M. (2024). "Not Every Use of AI Needs a Governance Policy; How Can You Tell the Difference?" *Corporate Compliance Insights*. May.

Kasanoff, B. (2014). "Are Real Estate Brokers Obsolete?" *Forbes Magazine*. April.

Kenton, W. (2024). "Human Resources (HR): Meaning and Responsibilities." *Investopedia*. August.

LawGeez. (2018). Comparing the Performance of AI to Human Lawyers in the Review of Standard Business Contracts. *LawGeez.*

Lee, K. (2021). "The Third Revolution in Warfare." *The Atlantic*. September.

Leitch, C. (2023). "25 Jobs That Will Disappear Thanks to AI." *Career Addict.*

Looker, R. (2024). "Trump Falsely Implies Taylor Swift Endorses Him." *BBC News.* August.

Lutkevich. B. (2024). "Will AI Replace Jobs?" *TechTarget.* November.

Marr, B. (2016). "What Is Affective Computing and How Could Emotional Machines Change Our Lives?" *Forbes Magazine.* May.

Martin, R. and Johnson, S. (2023). "Introducing NotebookLM." *Google.* July.

McKendrick, J. (2021). "Training Upward: Your Executives May Not Fully Understand Digital Transformation." *ZDNET.*

Merica, D. and Swenson, A. (2024). "Trump's Post of Fake Taylor Swift Endorsement Is His Latest Embrace of AI-Generated Images." *ABC News.*

Mesnard, X. (2016). "What Happens When Robots Take Our Jobs?" *World Economic Forum.* January.

MindManager. (2025). "Linear Thinking: The Ultimate Guide to the Linear Thought Process." *MindManager.*

Morgan Stanley. (2024). "AI and Cybersecurity: A New Era." *Morgan Stanley.* September.

Nam, J. (2023). "56% of College Students Have Used AI on Assignments or Exams" *Best Colleges.* November.

Narciso, E. (2015). "5 Reasons Millennials Aren't Buying Insurance from Local Agents." *ALM Property Casualty 360.* September.

NIST. (2023). "AI Risk Management Framework." *NIST.*

O'Shaughnessy, K. (2025). "ERP Strategy: What to Keep in Mind Before Taking the Leap." *SelectHub.* April.

Paloalto (2025). "What Is AI Governance." *Paloalto Networks.* January.

Panetta, K. (2016). "The CIO's Biggest Digital Transformation Challenges." *The Gartner Group.*

Pointing, C. (2024). "Where Are You, McPlant? Why McDonald's Still Doesn't Have a Meatless Option in the US." *VegNews.* April.

Qlik. (2025). "AI Readiness Lags Ambitions: Survey Highlights Key Gaps Threatening Generative AI Success." *Qlik.* March.

Rodgers, J. and Thomas, W. (2025). "How Internal Audit Can Govern AI Risks and Promote Compliance." *EY.* March.

Rosenbaum, E. (2015). "Retail Bank Branch is Doomed, and Banks Don't Know It." *CNBC.* June.

Saleem, F. (2023). "16 Jobs That Will Disappear in the Future Due to AI." *Insider.*

SCC. (2024). "Why Prompt Engineering Is the New Must-Have IT Skill." *SCC.* December.

Scott, M. (2024). "Deepfakes, Distrust and Disinformation: Welcome to the AI Election." *Politico.* April.

Snyder, B. (2015). "These Jobs Are Most Likely To Be Taken by a Computer." *Fortune Magazine.* May.

Sozzi, B. (2021). "McDonald's Automated Drive-Thru Is Just the Latest Sign of Robots Taking Over Fast-Food." *YahooFinance!* June.

Spark, S. (2019). "Artificial Intelligence Is Becoming Better Than Human Expertise." *HackerNoon*. March.

Spring, M. (2024). "Trump Supporters Target Black Voters with Faked AI Images." *BBC*. March.

Talin, B. (2024). "What Is a Digital Ecosystem? – Understanding the Most Profitable Business Model." *More Than Digital*. March.

The Black Vault. (1997). "DARPA's Research on Brain-Computer Interfaces." The Black Vault Via the FOIA Request. *The Black Vault*. May.

Twin, A. (2024). "Marketing in Business: Strategies and Types Explained." *Investopedia*. July.

University of Florida. (2015.) "Facilitative Decision-Making." *University of Florida Training & Organization Development.*

University of Oxford. (2019). "AI Early Diagnosis Could Save Heart and Cancer Patients." *University of Oxford*. January.

Verma, P. (2023). "The Rise of AI Fake News Is Creating a 'Misinformation Superspreader'." *The Washington Post*. December.

Wendling, M. (2024). "AI Can Be Easily Used to Make Fake Election Photos." *BBC*. March.

Wikipedia. (2025a). "Affective Computing." *Wikipedia*.

Wikipedia. (2025b). "The Singularity." *Wikipedia*.

Wikipedia. (2025c). "Digital Transformation." *Wikipedia*.

Zewe, A. (2023). "How Do Powerful Generative AI Systems Like ChatGPT Work." *MIT News*. November.

Zhang, M. (2024). "Top 10 Cloud Service Providers Globally in 2024." *Dgtl Infra*. April.

Zuboff, S. (2019). *The Age of Surveillance Capitalism: The Fight for a Human Future at the New Frontier of Power*. Hachette Book Group.

# Index

For Product Safety Concerns and Information please contact our EU
representative GPSR@taylorandfrancis.com
Taylor & Francis Verlag GmbH, Kaufingerstraße 24, 80331 München, Germany